also from
clearing skies press

Keeping the Baby Alive till Your Wife Gets Home

Keeping Your Toddler on Track till Mommy Gets Back

*Keeping Your Grandkids Alive till Their Ungrateful
Parents Arrive:* The Guide for Fun-Loving Granddads

Motherhood Exposed: Surviving Myth Conceptions
of Postmodern Parenting...through Good Times and Bad

. . . .

visit us online

clearingskies.com

Cover design by Ed Cahill

Distributed by Independent Publishers Group

Keeping the Baby Alive till Your Wife Gets Home

Special Edition

⌐   ⌐   ⌐   ⌐   ⌐   ⌐   ⌐

Walter Roark

Illustrations by Jason Snape, Michael Carney and Meghan Roark

clearing skies press

a clearing skies press original, Special Edition. October, 2005.
Copyright © 2005 by Walter Roark

Clearing Skies Press   4002 Dunbarton Way   Roswell, GA 30075
770-518-8931   visit us @ clearingskies.com

ISBN-13: 978-0-9707937-4-4
ISBN-10: 0-9707937-4-X

.   .   .   .

.   .   .   .

Publisher's Cataloging-in-Publication Data:

Roark, Walter.
        Keeping the baby alive till your wife gets home :
        special edition / by Walter Roark.
--1st ed.
 p. cm.

1. Fatherhood.   2. Parenting--Humor.
3. Father and infant.   4. Parenting   I. Title

HQ769.R63 2005   649'.122

10 9 8 7 6 5 4 3 2 1

Despite every effort to provide the reader with accurate, authoritative, indispensible information, the publisher and author can accept no responsibility whatever for loss, injury, slobbered-on turtlenecks and/or abusive behavior inflicted upon any parent using this book, by any baby, especially one who disagrees with its content.

Dedication

Thanks to little Meghan for
helping make this book possible;
and a special thank you to my wife,
Susan, for helping make Meghan

And now my life has changed in oh, so many ways...
Help! I need somebody, Help! Not just anybody. Help!
You know I need someone. Help!

—The Beatles

Table of Contents

Chapter three

Chapter four

Chapter five

Chapter six

Chapter seven

Chapter eight

Chapter nine

You Poor Mother, You

an introduction

⌐   ⌐   ⌐   ⌐   ⌐   ⌐   ⌐

This guide was created for the undertalented, unappreciated pinch-hitting utility man of team parenting—the modern father. It's for you if you're going to be or have already become one. It's for you because, as you'll soon find out, or may already suspect: you're expected to perform (and conform) to a new standard.

So if you've yet to acquire a 21st century attitude about the fine art of fathering, you had better start brushing up.

[1]

Most of all, this guide is for you because you really need help. The kind you won't find in baby magazines or ordinary infant care books. Why? Because they weren't designed or written for you. After all, you're not really a real mother. In your finest moments you're still a surrogate of sorts...a clownish pretender...part-time impostor. And the whole world knows it.

So don't expect to get the truth from traditional sources because they're really not interested in giving it to you. Even if one of these nice people promises to be totally honest with you, she will still cover up the gritty reality of this business about baby care.

However, you'll discover this guide to be an unglossed look at the pitfalls of keeping your sanity while you're keeping Baby breathing. It's packed with insider tips designed to help you buy time until help arrives. Make no mistake, this is no pretty fairy tale with a happy ending.

Undisclosed, true-to-life facts of father-infant care are detailed here for the first time: the good, the bad and the ugly. The sweet gullibility about perfectionism and "the joy of fatherhood" is stripped naked. The unvarnished truths about infant tyranny are finally revealed.

Even frightening topics such as diaper-changing, drooling and insect-eating are dissected and thoroughly examined.

After reading this confidential account of real infant behavior, you'll have learned your lesson. All the timeless secrets and up-to-date sleight-of-hand necessary for father-infant survival. Everything you need to be a savvy second-stringer.

Then you'll be in a position to play things your way. You won't have to resort to empty excuses when your wife returns from an important business meeting. You won't subject her to humiliating responses like, "Sorry, Dear. Things just got out of control and I couldn't handle it. Maybe I'll do better next time."

With the straight fatherly facts under your belt, you'll be able to say:

"Hey, Baby. No problem. When it comes to the home team, I'm a clutch player. Want to see us play Pat-A-Cake?"

The Male Misconception After Conception

a prologue for all seasons

⌐   ⌐   ⌐   ⌐   ⌐   ⌐   ⌐

Your leading role during conception may have been quite gratifying for you physically and emotionally. To that good sport who lives in all of us, the infamous male ego, it must have seemed like the all-star event of the season.

It's probably true that you demonstrated sensational early form and winning instincts for the great challenge of Fatherhood ahead. We know your timing was good, anyway.

Like a professional making the perfect shot to win— you came through. With true grit, keen aim and grace under pressure, you pleased the critics with a performance of real championship caliber. For one brief, blinding moment you demonstrated god-like talent, the delighted crowd screamed your name, and you became a shining star of stars.

Well, that was last season, Jack.

So just in case your delusions of grandeur have gotten the best of you...

REMEMBER THESE TWO RULES OF SPORTS AND LIFE:
1) Nobody cares about yesterday's heroes
2) Old champions are a dime-a-dozen

BUT MOST OF ALL, REMEMBER THIS:
While your impressive past performance may have had a lot to do with your success in becoming a father—it has absolutely nothing to do with parenting. Unfortunately, after conception, younger fathers especially seem to be stricken with a false sense of self-esteem and competence.

On the other hand, second-time Dads and men past 30 usually view impending Fatherhood with the proper attitude. Namely, a highly refined state of fear and apprehension. The wiser, more mature father knows too well that conception is like a good poke off the first tee. It has little bearing on who leaves the final hole with the fewest number of strokes—and the most coins in his pocket.

[6]

Be assured that being a good father is the toughest challenge you'll ever face in life. With infants in particular, it's a course filled with threatening hazards, unfair lies and severe penalties for the slightest error.

Let's be honest. As an untested amateur with two left thumbs and an awkward stance, you're in big trouble. You're off balance. Out of your class. Up against a recognized talent—a mommy-professional with soft hands, deft touch and limitless patience—you don't stand a chance in head-to-head competition.

But keep reading and take in some excellent advice tailored especially for you. Aim for a gentle, caring approach as you develop a flair for father-style mothering. Learn how to think less like a man, more like a mommy.

With enough practice, you (just like me) can at least play to your natural handicap without embarrassing yourself. Or losing all your balls in the process.

Keeping the Baby Alive till Your Wife Gets Home

SPECIAL EDITION

3 New Chapters
4 New Illustrations
32 New Pages

UNLIMITED LAUGHS!

Walter Roark

Author of

Keeping Your Grandkids Alive till Their Ungrateful Parents Arrive:
The Guide for Fun-Loving Granddads

Chapter one

Birthing Suites Ain't Made for Babies

I hear babies cry...... I watch them grow
They'll learn much more.....than I'll ever know
And I think to myself .....what a wonderful world
Yes, I think to myself .....what a wonderful world.

—Louis Armstrong

⌐   ⌐   ⌐   ⌐   ⌐   ⌐   ⌐

Congratulations on the amazing news! That eye-blink moment when you first discover you're going to be a dad holds no rivals among life's wake-up calls. First or fifth time, age 20 or 49, you feel the surge of emotion like a thunderbolt. Split-seconds later, the eternal (mostly internal) questions crackle through a man's consciousness...

[11]

(1) "Am I ready for this?"
(2) "Will I be a good father?"
(3) "Can we really afford this?"
(4) "Why is this incredible feeling of joy mixed with so much fear?"
(5) "Is *Birth* as much fun as *Conception*?"

These doubts in your mind are your first sign that babies, in fact, do come naked, but just the same, they're wrapped up in a bundle of questions prior to delivery.

If Baby could hear your questioning, he or she would answer like so...

1) "Ready or not, here I come!"
2) "Sure you will, and good is great—you don't have to be perfect."
3) "Hope so, cause I'll be eating a lot for the next 20+ years."
4) "Wait till you see all of the trouble I'll be getting into during the toddler and teen years."
5) "I don't know about *Conception*, but *Birth* is no fun for any body...baby, nurse's aid, midwife, doctor, father or mother...but I've heard the results are pretty good once I'm potty-trained."

Sure, we're all unsure how we'll handle fatherhood. Even the second or third time, a new being in your care is a first-class challenge...whether you're rich or poor, short or tall, outgoing or introverted, cowboy or accountant. Like anything, confidence comes with practice. That's why the stork gives you so much time to prepare. From Birth Announcement to Birth is a long haul. And since he's hauling the goods, Mr. Stork is the only soul who knows when your D-Day (Due Date) really is.

Done in by the Due Date

First off, I'd like to know what this misleading talk about *nine months* is all about. Truth is, pregnancies are more like 40 weeks. Last time I looked, there were four weeks in every month. And I'm sure your wife will agree, by the time Mr. Stork decides to land, those 40 weeks seem more like 60.

Now, your doctor may think it's great fun to calculate your D-Day. He gets a chance to practice a combination of high-level calculus and quantum physics rarely taught in medical school. But the fact is, not even Einstein had a clue about babies' due dates. The equation is much too complicated for any human. Two separate times, Albert's wife begged him to peg a D-Day number. He tried. Both times, in the end, Al gave up, broke down, then slinked back to the physics lab in defeat.

The reason? No one can factor in the mysteries of menstruation, ovulation and conception. Way too many variables.

Yet physicians confidently (wink! wink!) pinpoint a birth-day as if they were Einstein reinvented. Should you believe them? Well...maybe, maybe not. Doctors are notoriously optimistic. They believe they can work miracles, and predicting an accurate D-Day would be almost as much of a miracle as the miracle of birth itself. Have you ever spoken to a husband whose wife delivered on her due date?

Your job, as daddy-to-be, is to smile, celebrate, and go along with the program as best you can. At the turn of the new century, the United Nations passed two resolutions for new fathers worldwide. Resolution Number 2000-10 says, "A man and wife expecting a child must attend coeducational birthing classes for a minimum of eight weeks in the middle of the gestation period." As chief procreator, you must not question the value of the birthing classes even though you will be forced to talk to total strangers about sexual organs, bathroom habits, puke, poop and placentas. Violators of this proclamation will be banned to their choice of leper colonies in French Guiana.

Resolution Number 2000-11 states, "A man and wife expecting a child must furnish the coming baby's living space in a level of style, decorative appeal and comfort far exceeding their own. This precious space, commonly called *the nursery*, must be perfect in every way whether you live in a mansion or a hut. You must labor(?) in the space every night after work for a minimum of four months, following your wife's blueprint." You must never complain about the time and money spent on this "project" through spilled paint, bloody cut, bruised ego or battered bank account. Project escapees will be sentenced to 10 years of arts & crafts classes escorted by their mother-in-law.

So you see, your due date really becomes your LOTS TO DO date. Better get busy. Because, as alluded earlier, your precious, pre-birth moments may be fewer than you think if your expert medical teammate fumbles the D-Day snap and you end up with less time on the play clock than he/she predicted.

⌐   ⌐   ⌐   ⌐   ⌐   ⌐   ⌐

[14]

Step Right up and Take Your Chances

But whatever you do, don't panic. There's plenty of time for panic. Instead take a calm approach to the social whirlwind of birth announcements in the shape of hailing e-mails and a monsoon of informative phone calls. Your partner and you will know that everyone is judging your communications skills. Be sharp, be polite, be succinct. Above all, let the turbulent forecast of baby showers and maternity apparel shopping expeditions glide through your calendar without a ruffle of concern.

You, in comparison, have it easy, and you understand that. All you have to do is be supportive night and day, and carry out the twin U.N. resolutions to the best of your abilities. Oh, and grin like a chimpanzee any time your workmates congratulate you on being "pregnant."

It will be easy to smile. Because any expectant father in his right mind has to be damn glad *she's* the one who's really pregnant.

Raging Hormones: in the Eye of the Her-we-can

One reason to be glad is the knowledge that your body won't be taken over by oceans of bubbling hot hormones. The hormonal flood causes aches, pains, nausea, fatigue, weight gain and violent mood swings. Other than that, it's pretty nice. The hormones are all about change, and in pregnancy, sometimes the winds of change come fast. So grab hold of a sturdy tree trunk and get ready to weather the storm. Your only other options are evacuation and barricading yourself in the basement. Both no good.

You can survive the hormone storm by helping your spouse see the hurricaneless, bright side of things. For her, radiate a "can-do," "let's make the best of it" kind of attitude. For example, one day she complains about having to pee every five minutes. Your response should be, "That's a good thing, Dear. Think about, through frequent use, how clean you're keeping the internal/household plumbing. Way to go!"

Or perhaps the raging hormones have her sleepless and battling insomnia. At this point, you can fluff her pillow behind her back, punch the remote control and treat her to a musical-comedy on cable TV. Staying upbeat, you say, "If this keeps up, just think how many classic movies Baby will already know and love before he/she's even born. We can lick this problem!"

On the other hand, take care not to overdo the, "We Can Do It!" mentality. For example your housemate may act tired all the time and take frequent naps on the couch. Let her rest. Don't rush home from work and bounce through the doorway, shouting, "Rise and shine, Sleepyhead! Let's tackle the nursery now, stay up past midnight, rip out the drywall, put up new boards and sand the seams smooth. Then tomorrow we can finish the wallpapering. LET'S SEIZE THE MOMENT! WE CAN DO IT, GIRL!"

You also might see your sweetheart craving unusual foods in unusual (large) quantities. Again, howling hormones are the cause. Your response should be consistent: a gallon jar of queen-size olives? *No problem.* Super-size fries and a fried apple pie? *You got it.* Sardines and fudge? *We can do that.*

Thanks to the hormonal tempest, she may suffer from flurries of 'morning sickness' morning, noon and night. This type of nausea is worse during the early months of pregnancy. During this time if you find yourself near the center of the storm, you may witness your spouse throwing up one minute and pigging out the next.

You may even begin feeling queasy yourself, or experience other 'sympathy' pains like backache, heartburn or irritable bowel syndrome. Just don't expect any sympathy for your sympathy pains, because your hormones are now off-duty, and everyone knows it. You peaked at conception. At this point the forecast for your next hormonal blossoming is somewhat foggy with a 60% chance of intermittent cold showers.

Think of pregnancy and gestation as a challenging but fun-filled (and educational) marathon. If you've already been through it, you know you and your sweetheart fare better when you pace yourselves. On some days when you find doubts sprinting in and out of your head, turn your thoughts to the milestones of the 40-week chase. Relive the thrill of hearing your baby's heartbeat the first time. Picture the magical moment you realized that fuzzy image in the ultrasound was a brand-new human being created, at least in part, by *you*.

No doubt, though, even cave-dweller dads of Cro-Magnon times had pre-birth uncertainties about fatherhood pulsing neath their thick skulls. Back to the future in the tension-filled 21st century, when the WE'RE PREGNANT headlines spread around town, you may have a strong-opinioned pal butt in with, "Hey, Man. That's cool and everything, but are you sure you *really* want a baby *right now* at *your* age?"

Do your best not to listen to doubters. Just the same, because doubts are natural, perhaps this is the perfect time to examine your aptitude for the trials of pregnancy, birth, and all things BABY. Indeed, having a child is read-all-about-it, headline news. It doesn't matter if your new addition happens to be adopted, in-vitro fertilized or created the old-fashioned way.

Take a few minutes from your crazy, new-dad schedule and put your readiness to the test. There's no time limit or deadline; your results won't be reported to the media. But your score will be given an official news-industry rating, so be sure to answer each question carefully. *Press* on and best of luck!

Born to Be Wild News-Flash for New Dads: "Pop" Quiz
(use a bookmark or hand to cover answers—no peeking allowed!)

Question:

Month Two. You volunteer to cook dinner for your ravenous wife. "Goody!" she says. "I want braised buffalo tongue, rare; pickled pig's feet and bananas, boiled peanuts & goat cheese, anchovy sorbet, and for dessert, chocolate moose." Should you?

(a) Call ahead to the zoo...make sure they have all the ingredients you need for tonight's menu
(b) Say, "Would you like that moose on the rare side, like the buffalo?"
(c) Tell her she should enroll in the Pregnant Chef's Program at Le Cordon Bleu, she's *conceived* the most brilliant flavor combinations in culinary history
(d) Ask her, "Honey, wait a minute, did you mean mousse with two s's or moose with two o's?"

[19]

The answer is
all of the above. I know, this is a rotten, tricky way to start the
test, but you have easier questions coming. Speaking of questions, the one thing you *can't* do is question her choices. Food
cravings can't be explained with normal male logic. However,
in this case, the progression of (a) through (d) displays masculine power-logic as its best, with (d) being the most important.

Question:

You and Mommy-to-be are at birthing class snuggled on the
floor in a nest of pillows and blankets. As the gut-wrenching
live-birth video concludes, the guy to your left faints, then
slumps toward you, throwing up on your shoes. Should you?

> (a) Grab him by the ear, lifting his head off your ankles
> (b) Wipe his mouth clean with your pillowcase, then
>   perform mouth-to-mouth resuscitation
> (c) Look over at his wife and say, "You might consider
>   looking for a new coach, ma'am. This guy's a loser."
> (d) Smile, look up at his wife and say, "Do you two
>   lovebirds eat at Taco Bell every Wednesday night?"

The answer is
(d). Eliminate (a)—your grip might fail using a slippery, post-
puke ear. Let his wife perform (b) if she can stomach it—the
man didn't have a stroke; he simply passed out. Why be con-
descending and judgmental with (c)? No need to anger the
birthing gods at any stage of pregnancy. (d) is the friendly
choice, showing that you're not only a good sport, but that you
possess the detective skills of a modern-day Sherlock Holmes.

[20]

Question:

Month Six. One day your wife looks in the bedroom mirror and casually asks, "Honey, do you think I look fat?" Should you?

> (a) Pretend you don't hear her
> (b) Say, "Absolutely. I would too if I had a big-old belly like that hanging over my shorts."
> (c) Say, "Compared to what?"
> (d) Say, "I've never seen you look more attractive. After all, there's so much *more* of you. You look so good you're practically glowing, purple-veined cellulite and all."

The answer is
<u>none of the above</u>. For your sake, I certainly hope you answered this trick question correctly. A few of us might be tempted to choose (a), but Expecting Father Edict Number One is *always listen to your wife*—no matter how illogical her thought patterns may seem. Logic? She'll tell you what you can do with your logic. Answers (b), (c) and (d) are insanely insensitive—no options for compassionate 21st century dads.

Question:

Your first baby shower is a joyous occasion. With every gift unwrapping you charm the crowd with comments like, "This couldn't be more perfect!" Then, in a momentary lapse over a duplicate audio monitor, you exclaim, "I think we already have one of these!" Immediately, should you?

(a) Crawl under the coffee table

[21]

(b) Cackle at the old hens, "Just kidding—can't you tell I'm joking? This is wonderful."

(c) Say to the gift-giver, "How 'bout handing over that receipt so we can get something we really need?"

(d) Slap yourself on the forehead, saying sincerely, "Whoops. Must've been thinking about my ex-wife and that baby shower a few years ago. Sorry. This contraption is great!"

The answer is

(b). At a shower it's vital that you stay focused. Never stop nodding your head, smiling and spewing compliments. Never imply that a gift could be unimaginative or a duplicate. (b), though an imperfect choice, might work. (a) is unmanly and unworthy, (c) is crude and (d) is cruder than crude.

Question:

Month Seven. Your mother-in-law's 'long' weekend visit now stretches to 10 days. You enter your den and find her hunched over the computer making a detailed *PowerPoint* birth plan for you and her daughter. What should you say?

(a) "Marge, I like your computer savvy—very nice work."

(b) "You know, they rent these workstations at the library in your hometown. Need train fare?"

(c) Growl, "How'd you steal my password, you old bat!"

(d) "Look out, Marge! There's a lethal, embedded virus in that application. By now, it's eating away at your white blood cells. Your only hope is to catch a plane to the Mayo Clinic, and we better pack fast."

The answer is
(d). Looking at the facts, the story here is simple. Only a certified wimp would choose (a)—*your computer/her birth plan?* No thanks. (b) is creative, but not very persuasive. Answer (c) accomplishes nothing but gets you in a pile of trouble with your spouse. Like a smart reporter, you're sure to have deduced (d) is correct.

Question:

News-Flash! After 13 hours of pacing the hospital halls, your wife is finally 9 centimeters dilated in the transitional phase of labor. You dab her brow gently. Suddenly she clutches your wrist and screams, "Get out of my sight, you scum-bag!" Should you?

    (a) Ask her if she would like some more ice chips
    (b) Fall on the birthing suite floor in the fetal position, sucking your thumb
    (c) Say patronizingly, "Honey-Bunny, I forgive you. It's the drugs and you have no idea what you're saying."
    (d) Ask the midwife if she can call an Exorcist—your wife is possessed

The answer is
(a). Truth is, you must witness transitional labor to know how bizarre it can be. When events spiral out of control, it's best to be calm. Hence, answer (a). This late in the game, there are no fetal positions allowed (even Baby is head-down and looking for daylight), so (b) won't work. (c) will get you labeled a chauvinist pig, and (d) will get the medical staff laughing about the *Idiot Dad in Birthing Suite D.* Not the legacy you dreamed of.

Question:

Month Eight. After weeks of late-night labor, Baby's room is still far from ready. Your sweetheart begins to panic. You walk in late from a brutal day at the office and find her atop a wobbly stepladder drilling holes for curtain rods. Should you?

> (a) Rowdily praise her, "Yes! Let the screwing begin!"
> (b) Hint she should stop this insanity by frantically flipping the light switch on and off
> (c) Tell her to wait a sec while you wrap her tummy in insulation material so the noise won't disturb Baby
> (d) Loosen your necktie and grab a Phillips head—you're screwed and soon to be screwing alone

The answer is
(d). Even rookie dads should nail this multiple choice giveaway. (a)? Empty praise + vulgar little jokes get you nowhere... she's drilling 'cause you weren't there. (b) and (c) could frighten her into falling off the ladder, soon not to be a problem since you're going to take her place after correctly choosing (d).

Question:

Late Month Nine. Wintertime. Your dear heart's water breaks at 3:00 a.m. and suddenly you're driving 90 miles an hour to the hospital, running red lights and having a heart attack. She's having major contractions in the backseat. Should you?

> (a) Crouch on the floorboard with your hands clasped, crying softly to yourself
> (b) Open the window, stick your face out in the frosty air and scream, "You'll never catch me, Coppers!"

[24]

(c) Glance back and gently inquire, "This wouldn't be false labor, would it, Dear?"

(d) Look at her facial contortions in the rearview mirror, saying, "Listen, if push comes to shove do you think you could put this action on hold for half an hour?"

The answer is

(b). Answer (a) is less than brilliant since you're the pilot of this perilous mission. What would Captain Kirk think? Answers (c) and (d) would only earn you a swift kick to the head, sending you back to the idiocy of (a). On the other hand, (b) lets you release pent-up tension while keeping you alert for the balance of the terror-filled drive.

END OF TEST SCORING

Award yourself ten for each correct answer. If you cheated, award yourself zero. Either way, ratings are 100% official.

Born to Be Wild News-Flash for New Dads

Score	Official Rating
0	Exposed Plagiarist
10	Unpaid Intern
20	Copy Boy
30	Cub Reporter
40	Hardboiled Hack
50	Respected Journalist
60	Scud Stud
70	Combat Zone Hero
80	*ANCHORMAN*

[25]

Birth-Bag Bulletin: The Right, Wrong and Really Wrong

Rule Number One: With the exception of raw meat and frozen desserts, everything in your go-to-the-hospital luggage should be packed by Week 35.

Rule Number Two: By Week 35, if you have to choose between (a) plastering Baby's Room and (b) packing the hospital bag, don't hesitate, choose (b).

Making a List, Checking it Twice...

Definitive opinions from worldwide pregnancy experts on birth-bag items you may be considering:

Sugar-Free Lollipops (use these and ice chips to help keep your sweetie-pie's mouth from getting dry and her lips from getting chapped)   RIGHT

Lotion (soothing body massages...nice gestures till transitional labor when they beget violent behavior)   RIGHT

Music (her favorites...classical for calm, rock for screaming, hip-hop for a better birthing suite beat)   MAYBE

Laptop (Internet access or not, forget bringing office work—or games—with you to the hospital)   WRONG

Bullhorn (you're the coach, but you can't pace around barking orders like it's football practice)   REALLY WRONG

Toy (a gift for Baby, not for you)   RIGHT

This Book (Inappropriate and uncalled for, this fun-filled guide isn't designed for prime birthing time)   WRONG

Toolbox or Briefcase (Not even to hold your birth plan; all things work-related stay home)   REALLY WRONG

Stopwatch (the essential tool—wear it around your neck like a track coach, but leave the whistle at home)   RIGHT

Pillows (she might appreciate having a few extras, just like birthing class)   RIGHT

Camera (keep it simple, Hollywood this is not)   RIGHT

Sit-Com Videos (even the most hilarious episodes won't work—it's no laughing, pre-Baby matter)   WRONG

Sleep Mask & Earplugs (birth is the ultimate reality show: it's raw, unrehearsed and totally chaotic. It demands your 100% attention every second—no sleep for Mommy = no sleep for you till *The Stork Lands*)   REALLY WRONG

Birth...a Far Cry from Conception

The birth of your beautiful offspring, compared to the pleasures of planting your seed, comes far down the timeline and is a far different experience. Indeed, the glory days of conception are a sweet memory. But instead of thinking about exciting lovemaking in erotic locations, you're soon to be obsessed with epidurals, the Apgar Scale, episiotomies, and breastfeeding (your offspring, not you).

Yet, however close you were at conception (real close, anatomically speaking), and regardless of labor room medical terminology, sharing the birth experience should bring you and your mate infinitely closer. You might even look back on this 40-week span as a labor of love. Eventually.

Until that moment, prepare yourself for a virtual earthquake of uncontrollable lifestyle changes. Forevermore your old life will be past tense. The pets you doted on and treated like children will revert back to pets. Any and all your favorite hobbies will pale in relevance. The pain and elation of birth will help prepare you for a new truth: nothing will ever be as important to you as your child, nothing again in your lifetime.

My simple advice is 1) keep your common sense and 2) keep your sense of humor. When you start to take parenting too seriously, you can squeeze the joy right out of it. Have some fun. Squeeze Baby instead.

Most of all, skirt the trap of trying to be the perfect dad. It's impossible. Do the best you can every day and laugh at yourself along the way. Trust me. The pursuit of perfection is best left to saints and superstars.

Meanwhile...are you ready to take a look at how funny and imperfect life after birth can be?

Chapter two

Home from the Hospital

(A Star Is Born)

All Quiet on the Set...a dream beginning:

You're a happy new father with wife and offspring safe and secure on their first magical night home from the hospital. You drift into restful sleep.

Soon you're dreaming you're a world-famous Hollywood director having a dream. In this vivid fantasy, you're on the set of your latest movie and everything is going splendidly. Best of all, it's a very light schedule today and this particular set is the quietest, most peaceful one you can remember. So quiet you begin to feel uneasy. As if you know some nameless calamity leers menacingly, just on the other side of the calm.

Suddenly, your famous director's dream turns into the world's worst nightmare. You know it's a nightmare except the sound is blasting, special-effects stereo and some jerk has punched the treble so high you feel like your eardrums will rip. You must be on location filming a new multi-disaster adventure.

SCENE A: BANG! FLASH! HONK! You hear a fire truck, siren wailing, echoes racing down a dark city street... horn blasting, red-flashing machine skidding to a stop just outside your bedroom window. You wake, shouting, "FIRE! FIRE! FIRE!"

SCENE B: No—it's the roar of a falling 777, nose pointed at your rooftop—the ear-drilling scream engulfing your brain as the jet hurtles closer. You dive under the blanket bracing for the crash...knowing this is the end. But just in case this really is a movie, you cry (muffled), "Cut! Cut! Cut!"

Wait! This is no dream. YOU ARE AWAKE...you sit up, blinking, wondering why your ears won't stop throbbing. Finally, your consciousness returns. You're no high-powered Hollywood director; you're just an everyday new Dad. You're lying in bed listening to the desperate, wrenching bleats of your beautiful newborn babe...a tiny miracle fresh from the womb—a perfectly vulnerable, incredibly innocent three days old.

This means, roughly speaking, you're just 97 or so days away from a good night's sleep. That is, if you're lucky with the colic.

Colic: The Unsolved Mystery

What causes colic in a newborn? Well, the truth is, no one really knows. I realize that seems odd, considering today's deep well of medical-scientific knowledge. Yet this remains a mystery of the first magnitude, a true baffler. When colic was the case, even the greatest father-detectives of all-time didn't have a clue.

Sherlock Holmes? After twins with colic, he retired and took up an addictive drug habit. Charlie Chan? He gave his colicky baby boys numbers instead of names. The word is, before battling infant colic, a well-groomed, articulate Columbo wore designer trench coats and tooled around town in a spit-polished Cadillac coupe.

About all doctors will say is that colic has something to do with Baby's stomach. Thank you. That is certainly enlightening. As a Father, you'll soon discover colic has a lot to do with SCREAMING and UNHAPPINESS and HOWLING and ANGER and BAWLING and SUFFERING and SCREECHING and PAIN and SQUALLING and EXHAUSTION and NOISE and all-around MENTAL ILLNESS.

Oh, and the thing doctors don't say is that approximately 99.6% of all sampled infants have colic. But who knows. Like I said, maybe you'll be unusually lucky.

⌐ ⌐ ⌐ ⌐ ⌐

The Awakening

Getting Your
Father Act Together

So we already know you're likely to get at least a taste of this scourge called colic. But overall, what part should you play during this awkward time? How can you best help your wife care for this beautifully fragile being that you helped create—and are now responsible for?

Should you work quietly behind the scenes, giving support ($) and advice, settling disputes, offering assistance ($) on a regular basis? You know, sort of an "executive producer" type. After all, that's the most important part you've played so far.

Or should you start setting the stage for a dramatic new approach to the old standards of Father-Infant care?

Should you bounce onto the scene with electrifying energy, innovative ideas and snappy enthusiasm? Saying brightly, "Hey! I'm a co-star in this show, a real up-and-comer (so to speak). Give me credit—let me take charge for the day. I'll be such a hit, I know you'll be proud!"

As an intelligent, devoted new parent (who also happens to be grossly undertalented) what, exactly, do you believe your new role should be? That is, without making a spectacle of yourself, how can you contribute?

[34]

The answer is simple:

STAY OUT OF THE PICTURE!

Still a non-believer? Do you still find yourself insisting on taking part at this time? Then let me explain it to you again in cold, cutthroat, Hollywood-studio style.

You've heard of the star system? Good. Pretend you're not a star. In cinematic terms, understand what a genuine hit is—a true blockbuster? Okay. Make believe you're involved in a Grade C horror flick that's going straight to the bargain bin.

No, being a new father is not like being a star and playing a career part in a box office smash. It's more like being a hard-working character actor who gets good reviews but little publicity.

As Dad, you're the guy with the familiar name nobody can seem to remember. You did a fine job in a brief scene a few months ago, but now no one notices you on the set. You still have a few lines to speak, but you're not quite sure when you'll be called. All you know is someone in charge asked you to hang around just in case something comes up. Perhaps an action shot that requires a strong, father-figure type.

You said, "Sure. I'll be happy to help. What do you need?"

The person in charge said, "Well...nothing right now. Just sort of step over to the side, you know, out of the way for the moment. Keep your pants on and stand there in case we need you. Or your wallet."

Please understand. There's no pleasure in reviewing this depressing Daddy debut. It's not easy being brutally honest to a fellow father. Especially those of you who dreamed of being sensitive and involved and respected on the postpartum scene.

But be patient. This humbling experience will pass. Sooner than you think, someone in your home will recognize you and call you by your real name. Of course they'll probably just ask you to empty the diaper pail. But that's okay. When the time comes, you'll be glad to do it.

But what about the poor guy who can't ignore his own eagerness to get into the act? If this is you, then at least do your family a favor and have someone ask you the following questions about basic newborn care.

Think of it as a type of screen test designed to weed out bad home-from-the-hospital performances.

If you answer eight out of ten questions correctly, tell your test-giver you demand star treatment—you're brilliant. Between you and me, though, any Dad who gets eight right is either 1) dishonest, 2) a man with a dangerous attitude or 3) too smart to enjoy making a nuisance of himself anyway.

Readers unable to enlist a reliable test-person should consider placing a book marker below questions so that answers are covered. This will help those blindly ambitious souls tempted to peek.

Special Screen Test for Ambitious New Dads

Take 1: One medically approved, proper way for a new father to hold Baby securely is much like a fullback carrying a football.

True or False?

Answer: True. The key word is "securely." Even though you may feel like a fullback cradling a pigskin, the difference is, there are no fumbles allowed on this gridiron—no matter how many carries you make.

Take 2: With dramatic flourish, the clever thing to do is offer to change Baby's diapers within 24 hours of his/her homecoming. (Preferably in the presence of visiting relatives and neighbors.)

True or False?

Answer: False. A shocking display like this is unwise and out of character. You could be stuck in the role of boot-licking sidekick—doing new damage to your old heroic image. Instead be fair and business-like, privately offering to change Baby if your wife will change the oil in the station wagon.

Take 3: Immediately after birth Baby demonstrates the ability to communicate with a number of distinctive "cries."

True or False?

Answer: True. The "distinctive" cries go like this:
a) nerve-grating whine
b) numbing, obnoxious wail
c) full-tilt, brain-piercing shriek

They mean Baby is:
a) awake
b) awake and unhappy
c) awake, unhappy and hungry

Take 4: After twenty minutes of trying (and failing) to dress your three-week-old in a tie-string nightie, you should give up and call your wife for help.

True or False?

Answer: False. As you will soon discover with infant clothing (dozens of ties and snaps in the strangest places), it often requires twenty squirming minutes to figure out which strings match which.

Take 5: The effective, fatherly way to cope with a newborn's colic-induced screaming is to walk up to your wife with an armful of Maalox, Di-Gel and Pepto-Bismol, saying, "Would any of these be of help, Dearest?"

True or False?

Answer: True. From now until voting age, if your offspring becomes ill, this frightening yet innocent gesture should clear you of any responsibility or involvement.

Take 6: A newborn's favorite sound is its parent's voice.

True or False?

Answer: False. After listening to Baby for a few days, with the aid of fiendish inventions such as the wireless-remote infant audio monitor—you won't have any doubt about whose voice is his/her favorite.

Take 7: A proven method to protect yourself against Baby's frequent spit-ups is to place a cotton diaper or towel over the shoulder.

True or False?

Answer: False. The only way you can live at home and escape the effects of Baby's continuous discharge is to wear a full-length raincoat or plastic shower curtain refashioned as a cape.

Take 8: Upon observing your greedy offspring breast-feeding for the sixth time in one day, you have a sudden compulsion to cry out, snatch Baby away and take his/her place. Is this overreacting?

True or False?

Answer: True. Yes, this is a logical response for any sensitive man in touch with his true feelings. On the other hand, it's not too smart since it would most likely give your wife a heart attack. Repeat one hundred times: "No breast strokes allowed till Baby's old enough to swim. No breast strokes allowed till Baby's old enough to swim."

Take 9: Baby is just four weeks old; your wife comes to you suddenly in an aggressive, romantic mood. You should respond by ripping off your clothes, shouting, "Hallelujah!"

True or False?

Answer: True. This type of behavior is entirely appropriate since, according to surveys on the subject of postpartum depression, you are undoubtedly the luckiest man alive.

Take 10: One weekend you're out trimming the hedges and your wife calls you into the bathroom and asks if you're ready to try your first bath with Baby. Excitedly, you should switch the electric trimmers on and off, answering, "Wow! Sure! Can we play submarine, too?"

True or False?

Answer: True. At once, this response should project lasting impressions about your level of maturity, common sense and mental balance. All of which should keep you out of the bathroom and in the backyard where you belong.

END OF TEST

So how many correct answers did you record? If you scored below 70% (a failing grade), you're probably normal. Don't worry. Posting 70% or above suggests that you may be taking too seriously not only the test itself, but most likely your parental role as well.

I know, parental flunky or not, true flunking's still hard on the delicate psyche of any new sire. Let's just hope our special screen test has answered any questions you might have about your newborn ineptitude. You're probably disappointed, especially if you attended (as I did) one of those decidedly unnatural 'natural childbirth' classes. There they teach you that a father can play a major role straight out of the birthing suite. The instructor feels sorry for you, so she fills your head with pleasant propaganda designed to put you at ease and boost your confidence.

Well, this is merely a myth women create to help prop up our poorly constructed, gullible male egos. So what if they blend vital careers and perfect mother-care competence and still have enough time to sympathize with our trivial ego problems. Who needs that kind of compassion? Is self-esteem all that important?

I say we should take this beating like men. Admit new-age daddying is a hoax and get back to being our old-fashioned selfish selves. Why should we try to hog the scene when, in every direction, we run the risk of stepping on Mommy's lines and crippling the entire production?

Together, we should face the truth. We need to forget about grabbing headlines and being a hero and recognize reality:

Baby is the one and only star on this set.

So just keep to yourself for about three months. Stick to the den. Mow the yard. Go fertilize something like roses, for a change of pace. Work overtime when you can (it won't hurt—whether you're making money or just a good impression.)

Above all, now is the time to learn...

The Art of Being Anonymous.

⌐   ⌐   ⌐   ⌐   ⌐

The Art of Being Anonymous

Chances are, your mother-in-law will be running the household. Unless you have a keen interest in getting to know her more intimately, this is the best reason I can think of for you to take a bow and step out of the way for now.

The good news is your chances of achieving temporary anonymity get a major lift from the moment of your child's birth. Because—whether you like it or not—you will begin to lose your former identity. The first step seems to be an automatic, irreversible name change. Whereas previously you were known as Bob, Frank, Joe, or some reasonable equivalent, for the rest of your life this will become a rarely used professional pseudonym.

Your new name will be something like "Dad," "Da-Da," "Daddy," "Daddy-O," "Daddykums," "Pa," "Pop," "Pops," "Papa," "Poppy" or "Pap-Pap." Much later it will become simply, "Old Man." Don't expect to be called something dignified such as, "Father." For you, the unknown parent, dignity is a quality of the past...one you'll remember fondly after you slip into obscurity.

But for a few weeks, at least, you can pretend not to understand this bizarre transformation and make it work to your advantage. In other words, at home only answer to your true name when you feel like it. That way when you're hiding out somewhere in the apartment and your mother-in-law is looking for meaningful conversation, you can ignore her calls.

Later just say, "Gee, I'm sorry. I certainly didn't realize you were speaking to *me*."

Yes, it's a little sad, but so true. All the while Baby is busy developing his/her personality...you're deeply involved in losing yours. However, this is a change you will learn to welcome with time.

Being a modern parent means being tolerant, loving, sensitive, informed, intelligent and totally confident. Male or female, learning to be perfect won't leave you any time for a personality, anyway.

⌐   ⌐   ⌐   ⌐   ⌐

Last-minute tips on anonymity and a happy post-partum home life (birth to twelve weeks):

You may want to make a copy of these and tape them to the interior of your briefcase or toolbox. In every case, these critical reminders will steer you right. Trust them.

DO stay late at the office as often as you can. This is always well accepted, considering your new financial burden.

DON'T bore work mates with repeated stories and multiple photo sessions. One presentation each is all that is required (or desired). Put the video in a vault so it won't frighten your offspring when he or she reaches grammar school age.

DO offer to run to the store for diapers, formula, wipes, powder, lotion or (adult) aspirin as soon as you arrive home from work. Monitoring and restocking these essentials on a daily basis can be one of your more dynamic roles.

DON'T question the cost of any baby-related product.

DO compliment your mother-in-law on every meal she is involved in even if it gives you acute gastritis.

DON'T, under any circumstances, ever inquire about the length of your mother-in-law's "visit."

DO tell your wife how beautiful she is at least three times a day because she may be suffering from depression, and so will you if you don't.

DON'T mention sex or the lack of it to anyone for any reason. Better yet, stop thinking about it altogether.

DO start a project in the basement or take up a new hobby to help you pass the time and stay out of the way.

DON'T waste time preparing a financial plan for your child's future or education. Your mother-in-law will present hers to you when she's ready.

DO surrender to mob scene (or obscene) gatherings of overnight relatives, giving them full control of cable/satellite programming without comment.

DON'T read the Entertainment section of the newspaper. Also, avoid Internet sites with critical reviews of stage or film. You will not be seeing theater or first-run movies for a very long time.

DO purchase a small black & white television with rabbit ears. Plan to watch it alone as your wife will be busy and your houseguests will not like sharing the big-screen.

DON'T even think about Internet access. If it's urgent, your brother-in-law will let you check your e-mail after 11:00 p.m.

DO smile frequently and happily accept your new role as a non-person.

Chapter three

Poopies: a Sticky Situation from Top to Bottom

Perhaps even before your three-month period of near isolation is completed, you will be forced into a dangerous confrontation with the most frightening reality of your new lifestyle. Of course, I am talking about the final outcome of your growing offspring's voracious appetite.

As second-string coach pacing the infant care sidelines, you've been near the action, but never in the thick of it. Yet this short season of observation should have given you time to read, to reflect, to embrace the great body of wisdom and fathering philosophies of an enlightened age. After all, you're no different than any other 21st century dad. You're capable. And willing. Plus you've already made your mark—performing admirably throughout the rigors of conception and birth.

The only question is, are you prepared?

Known officially as parental unit number two (how cruel, considering the subject), you will soon share the responsibility for life's ultimate cleaning chore. The end result (you might say) of Baby's eager attachment to the very breasts you once knew and loved.

Yes, I realize from hands-on experience how terrifying this topic can be. Yet it has to be discussed, disgusting or not. You simply have to prepare, because if you fail this critical test of your daddily aptitude, you may never recover to father again.

Did I say test? More than that, it's literally a study of your intestinal fortitude, an intense examination of your self-control, a certain measure of your manhood.

What's worse, your wife will never understand your feelings about this subject. She would just think you were being silly if you told her about being afraid. So don't. To her cleaning a baby's behind is as normal as changing a sparkplug or taking out the garbage. You and I know that's ridiculous. But she'll never share your anxieties, so keep them to yourself. Besides, it's only a matter of three or four years before your diaper pail days are over.

One sunny Saturday afternoon when Mommy is out and you're in charge, Baby will deliver a message that can't be ignored. Ready or not, sink or swim, you and your diaper-changing wits will be fully tested. Take the following advice to heart and you'll be able to function in a calm, masculine manner. Quicker than you can say, "Up-chuck," you and your offspring will put this problem behind you.

Keep practicing and you'll soon be enjoying breakfast again with confidence.

The Poopie Encounter: a Man's Approach

Before you face the inevitable, begin prepping for your first encounter by observing your wife in action. Her command of cool, effortless skill is something you could never hope to achieve, but you have to start somewhere. Keep in mind also that you should NEVER try to imitate her unique technique. That brand of arrogance could get you into very deep...well, trouble. Your purpose in the beginning is merely to become comfortable with the setting.

First, always position yourself on the end of the changing table closest to Baby's head. This is important. Concentrate at all times on his/her face only, breathing through your mouth if necessary—but quietly. Smile at your wife and act normal. Talk to the baby. DO NOT watch what your wife is doing. DO NOT look when she opens the diaper pail. If you follow these directions and still become desperately nauseous, simply put your hand over your mouth, pretend you have to sneeze, then promptly leave the room.

Condition yourself with the above procedure at every opportunity. Remember: try not to be squeamish, and never arouse suspicion about your true feelings. You must have discipline. At first, you may want to nonchalantly follow Mommy every time she takes Baby into the nursery. Otherwise you may miss practice sessions. After a few weeks, though, you'll be able to sense when an encounter is imminent.

Let's say you've had enough of basic training and think you're ready for the real thing. You believe you can perform under fire, so to speak, when the chips are down. Fine. Just don't volunteer. Duty will call soon enough and you'll get your chance.

Try thinking of yourself as a rookie quarterback in the NFL. They rarely play except out of necessity. Then they usually fumble the snap from center or throw an interception. With the subject at hand, you want to avoid a potentially humiliating scene such as that.

If you've planned everything perfectly, the call to action will come when you and Baby are all alone. Your wife is working or shopping and you have made it your mission to be physically conditioned, well-coached and mentally prepared.

This means, like a smart rookie, you have the essential equipment on-hand and ready:

Diapers: convince Mommy early-on that solely for Baby's benefit, there will be no compromise in your household concerning diaper quality. Make certain each brand you buy has the following features:

> (a) Triple-improved, industrial-strength absorbency
>
> (b) One-step, no-fail, super-glue refastenable tapes
>
> (c) Leg-hugging, vise-grip, double-elastic gathers
>
> (d) Scientifically engineered waist leakage barrier

These characteristics are naturally available only with packaged disposable models. What about old-fashioned cloth diapers? I once told my wife we should consider them because I had read cloth is recyclable and friendly to the environment.

But then she explained to me (1) how many gallons of hot water and chemicals it takes to clean a load of cloth diapers and (2) the fact that they don't go straight from Baby to the washing machine or diaper service. The intermediate step uses more water...plus it's too vile and uncivilized to talk about.

Wipes: Never skimp on this item—it's your most important tool. Like a carpenter needs a good hammer, you need the best baby wipe money can buy. Generic brands are out. Look for size first (think BIG), followed by thickness, dependable pop-up/easy-access characteristics, easy foldability and consistent moistness. Let's face it, when the action gets hot and heavy you don't want to be caught standing there holding a tiny, dried-out, wimpy wipe, do you?

Room Deodorant: A smart investment you'll appreci-
ate. Spray it before you start for extra protection in case you
forget to breathe through your mouth for a few seconds. A
thick, overdone pine scent is nice.

Paper Towels: Again, you get what you pay for. Go for
the widest, thickest, most expensive roll available. Get a dozen.
Tell your wife you were driving by a store grand-opening and
they were giving them away.

Plastic Gloves: I'm talking about the tight-fitting type
homemakers used back in the days before automatic dish-
washers. I almost bought a box, but then I started thinking
about what would happen when you remove them after diapering. Can you imagine the sling-shot effect as you yank each
tight-fitting finger off? That image made me even queasier.
Now, a heavy-duty pair of cotton garden gloves...there's an
idea with promise.

⌐   ⌐   ⌐   ⌐   ⌐

Poopulation Control:
Doing Your Doodie

Standard Poopie Procedure, Step by Step

Step One: As soon as Mommy leaves the house, get your equipment in order and put everything within easy reach of the changing table.

Step Two: Relax. Your fate is in Baby's hands (or elsewhere) and he/she instinctively knows. Nervousness could create a condition called *premature poopulation*. This occurs when you become overly excited, rush into action and INTERRUPT Baby's normal function. This could be disastrous. YOU MUST exercise poopulation control.

Step Three: There is no need to closely observe or examine Baby for signs of readiness. Your rigorous training and highly refined senses will tell you when it's time. When you think you're sure, wait another five minutes.

Step Four: GENTLY carry child to changing table.

Step Five: For back-up security reasons, place Baby on a double-thick, double-wide layer of the special paper towels you so wisely purchased.

Step Six: Spray room with fresh fragrance, open diaper pail and spray it, too. Above all, DO NOT FAIL TO REMOVE LID OF DIAPER PAIL. Otherwise you'll be like a trapped quarterback—holding the ball with no place to go.

Step Seven: Take out a MINIMUM of five baby wipes and spread them carefully and separately on edge of table where Baby cannot kick them onto floor.

Step Eight: Cautiously undo refastenable tapes, grit your teeth and check to see if, in fact, you may still have gotten lucky, somehow. If not, proceed to Step Nine.

Step Nine: Begin clean-up (from the bottom up). To help control nausea, concentrate on a pleasant subject. Imagine yourself in a sunlit meadow or strolling through a majestic pine-scented forest. Recite the names and positions of all the players on the major league team you loved most as an eleven-year-old.

Step Ten: Painstakingly complete clean-up. If you've managed to avoid Baby's malicious kicking and squirming, quickly dispose of all appropriate materials in diaper pail and close the lid. Proceed to Step Eleven. If you've yet to achieve satisfactory results, initiate cleaning procedure with back-up paper towels, then repeat this step.
CAUTION: Work fast now and contain Baby's movements or your problem may spread like a wild brush fire.

Step Eleven: Powder and rediaper Baby.

Step Twelve: Congratulations! You can now put happy infant in playpen, hurry to the nearest bathroom and say good-bye to breakfast.

Emergency Poopie Procedure, ONLY

Step One: Follow Steps One through Eight of your Standard Procedure.

Step Two: If after investigation you feel you are totally losing control and the magnitude of the situation is something you cannot handle in the conventional manner, then—and only then—proceed with Emergency Step Three.

Step Three: Refasten refastenable tapes. Carry infant carefully into the closest bathroom. Fill the sink with warm water and locate an old washcloth and towel. Baby will think you are crazy and may become upset...so talk, tell jokes, sing or hum—do everything possible to keep him/her calm.

Step Four: EASE Baby out of diaper. Test water temperature before immersing his/her backside into sink. IMPORTANT: Unless you enjoy mopping up counters and floors with a high-powered disinfectant, be sure water level is appropriate. In this operation, there's no room for hindsight.

Step Five: Soak Baby's bottom with a gentle up/down dunking motion. Tell Baby this is a fun new game Da-Da has invented just for him/her. If at any time you determine infant's wide-eyed gaze to be true shock—immediately discontinue procedure. Otherwise, continue soaking until desired results are attained.

Step Six: Gently swab area of concern with the washcloth until all parts are perfectly sanitary. Avoid looking at results in sink.

Step Seven: Wrap infant in towel until he/she is warm and dry. Return to changing table for powdering and diapering.

Step Eight: You can now place clean but confused child in playpen, then return to bathroom for unpleasant clean-up (and throw-up if necessary). Dispose of all incriminating evidence.

Step Nine: If the bathroom cleaning detail demanded by emergency procedure hasn't already convinced you, make a solid commitment to yourself to try and follow standard procedure in the future.

Chapter four

Feeding a Face Only a Father Could Love

⌐ ⌐ ⌐ ⌐ ⌐ ⌐ ⌐

An obscure fact concerning the life of Sir Isaac Newton is that he proudly fathered ten offspring who helped him attach a pair of little known corollaries to his famous theory of physics:

First, the famous theory:

NEWTON's LAW of GRAVITY:
what goes up, must come down.

Now, revealed for the first time, Newton's brilliant, yet unknown twin corollaries to the physical science of father-infant care:

Newton's Corollary to Infant Feeding Number One:
*what goes
down, will come up.*

Newton's Corollary to Infant Feeding Number Two:
*what goes in,
must come out.*

In the last chapter, we gave full coverage, in every way possible, to Newton's Corollary Number Two (topic noted above). So let us now turn our attention to the cause and effect of Corollary One, as well as the mysteries of infant eating as a whole. Or should I say, as a general subject.

Anatomically speaking, the bottomless pit known as your baby's digestive system will achieve full human development around the age of three to four months. Prior to this juncture, Baby's eating habits will likely not concern you very much.

After all, Baby simply gorges himself/herself around-the-clock on your wife's free-flowing milk supply. That is why an infant's complexion is so perfectly smooth, unblemished and tender. Just like milk-fed veal in a good scallopini.

But if you're an emotionally mature father, this nonstop sucking routine will never annoy you in the least, nor cause even the slightest twinge of jealousy. So what if your wife has forgotten your name. You'll get to know each other again...someday.

Now is the time to think of the strong nutritional foundation your little one is building via Mom's mammaries. It's really a very beautiful thing. Not to mention relatively cost-free and convenient—qualities a mature father always appreciates.

Just the same, regardless of how mature you are, and whether you've experienced military service or not, nothing can prepare you for the upcoming battle on your calendar. The first introduction of solid food past the lips of your offspring is the trumpet call to arms.

No doubt your first instinct will be to play the hero. We're all heroes at heart. But resist, if you can, the urge to save the day, galloping in on your rocking horse like some green-horn calvary officer. The combat-savvy females around you will know better. They know you can't just charge into battle with an infant. Think about it. Even when their eyes are closed, ordinary babies can see you coming from miles away.

Your wife and her trusty allies will have the campaign planned. Part blitzkrieg, part espionage, part old-fashioned trench warfare. You can rest easy behind the lines, perhaps casually observing with your hunting binoculars. When the girls need it, you'll probably get called on to run a foxhole full of courier tasks. Otherwise, for your part, all will be quiet on the infant feeding front. At least in the beginning.

[61]

Then when you least expect it, when the female shock troops need a break most, you'll be thrown into action. Don't be too eager. Yes, combat is appealing to your sense of history and male pride, but this type of hand-to-hand fighting is different. It's dirty. It's unrewarding. Worst of all, there are no heroes.

When you're called to duty, General Mommy will take a minute to brief you and map out a strategy—probably some kind of murderous flanking maneuver around the side of the high chair. It won't be pretty. All any dad can do at this point is strap on his trench spade and hop into no man's land.

Good luck, pardner. Remember, take no prisoners. And don't forget to wear your splatter gear.

The War of Nutrition

The day will come when Mommy orders it's time to start Baby on solid foods. This usually occurs about the time she feels Baby's steel-clamp jaw power shifting from annoying to unbearable.

By the way, the term "solid" foods is very much a misnomer. What we're really talking about is ferment of lumpy, runny cereal made from dried oat or rice flakes. All you do is add your choice of liquid. Unfit for human or beast, this toxic slop was designed to increase *parents*' endurance at feeding time. Baby naturally refuses it—with vacuum-sealed lips impervious to assault by spoon, crowbar or laser gun. You, your wife, your relatives and other mothers in the neighbor-hood may be thrown into the battle. Baby will take on all comers, groups or individuals.

The scene will be littered with wrecked spoons, bibs, bowls and mounds of dried, caked cereals before he/she final-ly gives in from exhaustion. As a father, the brutality of this experience—the awful carnage—should fully prepare you to take flight in your very own solo feeding. Test the logic on stray pets if you like. You'll see. Once your child agrees to eat tasteless gruel rejected by a starving mongrel, he/she will eat practically anything.

Once the battle is won and the culinary path is clear, you'll be on easy street. You'll be dishing out jars of strained squash and green peas like a veteran. At that point all you'll need is a little common sense and a lot of patience.

But if you find your first attempt approaching and you still feel all alone and a bit inadequate, here's a simple test—another 'Pop' quiz—you may want to file as an impor-tant reference source in your parenting library.

(*Caution:* this informal examination and the scoring tips following it are for *fathers only*. That in mind, the idea of concerned wives *administering* the test to their husbands is an excellent one. While we endorse the concept of Mommy-scored quizzes, we ask respectfully that female test-givers avoid flaunt-ing their superior knowledge during and after the exam. Thank you for your understanding.)

'Pop' Quiz Number Two:
Solo Feeding

Question:

Everything is going fine until Baby decides to make poopies during the middle of dinner. Should you?

(a) Finish feeding, then change diaper
(b) Change diaper, then finish feeding
(c) Forget feeding, throw up on high chair
(d) Go hide in basement until help arrives

The answer is
(a). Part of being "parental unit number two" means trying harder. Therefore, (c) and (d) are unacceptable options. With (b), you run the risk of premature poopulation which could be traumatic as well as unacceptable.

Question:

Your wife is working; Baby is six-months-old and suddenly starving. After frantic searching, you find not an ounce of baby food in the house. Should you?

(a) Thaw out a nice T-Bone
(b) Put screaming infant in car; hurry to grocery store
(c) Jog to neighborhood day care center and beg for Gerber's
(d) Cower in the playpen and wait for a reply to your sobbing voice mail

The answer is
(b). Answers (a), (c), and (d) are simply too slow in this situation.

Question:

Feeding time is proceeding smoothly until Baby viciously grabs spoon, causing you to stuff fruit up his/her nose. Should you?

(a) Call a plumber
(b) Ask Baby how he/she likes them apples
(c) Search bathroom for ear syringe
(d) Continue feeding as if nothing happened

The answer is
(d). Although a good idea, (a) is just too expensive. (b) is an honest response, but not a very mature one. (c) would be the wrong tool for the job. (d) is the poised approach since babies are used to having food matter stuck in every orifice.

Question:

Your eleven-month-old is laughing uncontrollably because he/she just spit Spaghetti-O's all over your new argyle sweater. Should you?

(a) Compliment Baby on his/her terrific sense of humor
(b) Smile and say, "Gee, thanks for sharing"
(c) Be glad your sweater has an argyle pattern
(d) Cram a bib in his/her mouth and start laughing yourself

The answer is
all of the above. Psychologically speaking, answers (a) and (b) promote positive behavior, while answer (d) does a good job reinforcing the sense of humor concept in answer (a). (c) is just good common sense.

Question:

You feel terrible because you just burned Baby's tongue after forgetting to test bottle temperature and he/she is shrieking in pain. Should you?

>(a) Turn up stereo so the neighbors won't hear
>(b) Apologize to Baby and plead for forgiveness
>(c) Offer him/her a frosty mug of Heineken
>(d) Ignore infant, knowing he/she will seek revenge sooner or later

The answer is
(c). Answer (a) is purely inconsiderate; (b) is a complete waste of time. (c) is correct because not only do most babies love beer, but it may help him/her forget what happened. Answer (d) is a good choice and also very true— but (c) is still smarter.

Question:

Home from work after a mind-numbing commute, you stride into the breakfast nook where Aunt Mildred is spooning up chocolate mousse to your offspring. Should you?

> (a) Congratulate Auntie on ruining your
>   Anniversary Dinner dessert, then smile
>   and ask her to extend her 10-day visit
> (b) Splatter a handful of chocolate on the old
>   bag's cheek, quickly swipe "NO" on it
>   with your index finger
> (c) Tear the crystal dessert goblet from her
>   hands and scream, "That's MINE—back
>   off you old biddy!"
> (d) Bend down, go nose-to-nose with Baby
>   for a good, long stare. Announce now is
>   the time to learn the concept of sharing

The answer is

(a). Answer (b) would obviously waste more of a good thing. (c) is not worthy of you—too violent and adolescent. (d)? Well, the concept of (d) has appeal when you look at it on paper, but your offspring will only listen to "sharing" advice for one 24-hour period between the age of 7 and 8 years. Don't waste your breath now. (a) is right because it will throw Aunt Mildred off balance, plus it uses reverse psychology—always a great tool.

Question:

You turn the kitchen corner and discover your eight-month-old feasting from the beagle's bowl. Should you?

> (a) Stop feeding the dog and remove the
>   temptation
> (b) Stop feeding Baby since his/her diet is
>   nutritionally complete

(c) Acknowledge Baby's preference and switch
from Gerber to Gravy Train
(d) Have infant's warming dish engraved with
"Snoopy"

The answer is
<u>none of the above</u>. The mature father will realize this question was invented strictly for a cheap laugh. Besides, any parent knows when it comes to pet products, babies are primarily attracted to used kitty litter.

Question:

One Saturday in March you're feeding your beautiful bambino while watching the NCAA basketball tournament. A commercial comes on, you lovingly glance at Baby and notice his/her skin has turned a frightening shade of orange. Should you?

(a) Chuckle and say, "I told your mom we
should have named you *Spalding*."
(b) Start patting Baby on the head like you're
dribbling through the lane for a lay-up
(c) Make a note that Baby won't need a
Halloween costume in the fall
(d) Get up and go to the pantry for strained
peas, realizing you've unwittingly been
feeding the youngster a steady diet of
carrots for the past ten weekends

The answer is
(d). We all make mistakes, don't we? Perhaps you're fond (a)
of the name Spalding, but it was already used in a famous comedy film. Look out for (b)!—Baby's softspot won't permit it. (c)
is smart plus thrifty, but it doesn't really solve this problem.
You're right, (d) is a slam-dunk for the home team.

Scoring: Test-takers should be awarded ten points for each
correct answer. Then total the score and look for your rating
below.

Pop Quiz on Solo Feeding

Score	Official Rating
0	Shirtless Spectator
10	Waterboy
20	Reject
30	Rookie
40	Special Teams Sub
50	Second Stringer
60	Veteran
70	All-Pro
80	LEGEND

⌐   ⌐   ⌐   ⌐   ⌐

Typical Food Pyramid for the Average Infant

A Note on
Chronic Infant Drool

Unfortunately, mealtimes are not the only instance of recurring infant emission. The disgusting oral discharges (otherwise known as "burping up") that you experience during Baby's breast-feeding period are in later months replaced by a continuous saliva flow. This in-between-meal drooling may at first represent an almost welcome change. Then it will begin to drive you crazy—like a leaking faucet that can never be repaired. In a single afternoon, you may be compelled to swab Baby's chin forty to fifty times. This is completely normal.

Although "drool bibs" are available, I don't recommend them since they potentially promote a bigger mess. A clean-as-you-go method seems to be the best policy under the circumstances. You will of course need a generous supply of drool cloths for the job. This is where cotton diapers really do come in handy. But rather than keeping one on your person at all times (most unpleasant as the day wears on), simply place a cloth in a convenient (yet discreet) spot in every room.

Above all, keep your composure, knowing as with a terminal disease, the symptoms of chronic drool can be treated but never cured.

Most frustrating is the knowledge that you may never even be able to locate the source of the seepage. The worst thing you could do is strap on your tool belt...envisioning heroic deeds like those taught in plumbing school. It would be best to avoid altogether the image of a leaking faucet in your mind. You might develop an overwhelming urge to grab Baby's head and twist his/her ears clockwise, thereby shutting off the leak. This will not work.

If, in the unlikely event you find yourself with an infant who does not drool continuously, I suggest you take him/her to the nearest pediatric service center for an emissions systems check. There could be something stopped up.

Chapter five

Propagating Toys or Things That Go Hump in the Night

┘ ┘ ┘ ┘ ┘ ┘ ┘

One of the major challenges you'll encounter in caring for your child is how to avoid breaking your own neck when tripping over his or her ever-multiplying "educational" toys. Next to the piles of toys will lurk mounds of huggable, fuzzy animal friends that require more daddy detours.

Obviously you cannot be an adequate provider of love, care, proper supervision and/or financial support if you wind up bed-ridden by a crippling injury. Here, as never before, the phrase "Watch Your Step" digs deeply into the male psyche.

KEEPING THE BABY ALIVE TILL YOUR WIFE GETS HOME: Special Edition

Your instinctive uneasiness about the rumble and squawk of rolling doggies and flapping ducks is right on track. You don't have to be a Neanderthal to find buzzing bees and clapping clowns unsettling in your dwelling. You're not necessarily primitive because you don't love having little furry animals underfoot. And what about those sneering plush dinosaurs in aggressive neon colors? That's enough to bring out the worst fears in any prehistoric subconscious.

You can almost smell trouble coming. Even before your offspring arrives you are besieged by a bewildering array of toy peddlers offering their wares via Internet, newspaper, television, magazine, telephone, catalog, coupon, in-store and door-to-door solicitation. Adding to the onslaught in recent years are clever, premeditated e-mail 'edutorials' designed to snare innocent new moms and dads with modems.

Everywhere you turn, *they* have your number. *They* analyze everything from your bandwidth to your dirty clothes bin. They know what size bed you sleep in and how many bagels you eat when you get out of it in the morning.

To *them*, your wife's condition is like a beacon. It illuminates the mother of all numbers—your due date—for all to see and record. Soon dollar signs begin lighting in the eyes of every pitchman, huckster and sales promotion specialist from here to Timbuktu.

Mysteriously but surely, your good name begins popping up on marketing lists used by every infant-matériel manufacturer in the universe. Your electronic and streetside mailboxes, especially, overflow with irresistible offers.

[74]

You certainly don't have to be a marketing genius to figure out the facts. Even a cavemen could tell. These people want your money and won't rest until they have it. Even worse, they make you feel guilty if you don't give it to them. After all, the fruit of your loins could develop severe learning disabilities without the world's latest design in squeaking bunnies.

But the squeaking bunny, I'm afraid to say, is just the beginning of your torment and guilt.

Your home will soon be submerged in a flood of biblical proportions, a rising tide of plush animals that would discourage Noah himself. Get ready for a boatload of creeping, crawling, furry critters. Mice, monkeys, geese, puppies and ponies...whiskers, tails, feathers, paws and hooves...squeaking, chattering, honking, barking and neighing.

As a bonus, you'll discover each beast carries with it a name so incredibly cute your brain will pucker at the thought of pronouncing it. Rest easy. Your wife won't make you say their ridiculous names until Baby learns how, and that's a good hike down the road.

Did I mention bears? The first wave will be bears. Bears, above all, will hibernate in every corner of your baby's room. Why is that? Because bears are cute and cuddly. Bears have sweet facial expressions. As men, you and I know a real bear could rip the limbs off your infant and digest them through a long winter snooze. That's reality. Well, forget reality. It has nothing to do with the nutty, nutcracker fantasy world you live in now.

It won't take long till you acknowledge the insanity of it all. In your cluttered seascape, where toys swim freely room-to-room with an air of disdain, no longer do Dads rule. In your place, do-dads rule.

Nay, I say to you dear brother-Father, all you can do is pray that the coming packages be small rather than large. All things being relative, a tiny stuffed creature sent by Cousin Clem is better than a huge stuffed creature.

Ultimately, the misguided folks bringing you the bears and the other damn do-dads are the very people in control of the dam. Better get your waders on. They're about to open the floodgates on you.

⌐   ⌐   ⌐   ⌐   ⌐

Deliver Us from Evil

Beware of Relatives Bearing Gifts

Aggravating the situation ten-squared are the "little gifts" you'll be receiving over the next several years from thoughtful relatives. These zealous do-gooders see to it that Baby has a limitless supply of new and used toys, not to mention clothing.

The UPS man soon knows your address by heart. Daily you'll be delighted to find a new package sitting on your doorstep. One, no doubt, containing several stuffed toys, duplicate dolls, baseball bat or other essential. Of course this never-ending trickle is totally separate from the true gusher you get in person. The visiting relative without a gift is such a rare bird that it may as well be extinct.

From the very first prenatal "baby" shower until mid-adolescence, your progeny will be engulfed in an ocean of objects d' cute. Your wife will receive some gifts, too. What do you get? You get to figure out what to do with all this *stuff*.

This swirling undercurrent of mass consumption makes a mockery of your living landscape. Inside and out, your personal space erodes under the deluge. Like a man on a shrinking island you watch the tide of creeping toys lap closer.

At the same time, driving you to madness, Baby outgrows all items in a matter of days. Playthings and articles of clothing become obsolete at warp speed. Your offspring discards them or pops out of them, giving each a lifespan of approximately 26.4 days.

By the time your toy-bloated infant has marked his/her ten-month birthday, every room in your home will have an individual nest of unrestrained, self-multiplying characters—every nook a virtual breeding ground. Just as in the classic horror film, "The Blob," these threatening piles keep growing and growing and growing.

One morning you'll wake to the discovery that impossibly, almost overnight, the toys have taken over. The sheer volume and tangle of individual piles can be intimidating. And frightening, too—after dark. That's when you feel them stirring in the night, shadows against the wall, faintly moving in the moonlight. Then you reach the light switch only to find sweet doll faces and jacks-in-the-box staring innocently back at you. Except you're quite sure there are at least one or two new faces in the crowd.

So how do you keep your skin from crawling in the middle of the night? How can you be sure to protect yourself from personal accident, at the same time keeping pathways clear for normal traffic? As a combination doting parental unit and down-to-earth Da-Da, how do you battle (both bravely and creatively) this scourge of your household?

You fight dirty, that's how.

Start by discreetly eliminating any toy that has not attracted Baby's attention in over thirty days. Let's face it, some toys just lack star quality. And if they can't entertain like they're supposed to—then—all they deserve is a swift kick out the door. That's show business. The key is to let Baby decide who stays and who pays. This helps relieve any guilt feelings you may have later.

Choose a time when you and Baby are alone for at least an hour. Place him/her in a comfortable spot (high chair, stroller) and begin the auditions. Each toy should get about twenty seconds to show its stuff. If Baby shows displeasure or throws it down before time's up—the item's a goner. Put rejects in a box, mark it *Goodwill* or *Salvation Army*, then casually plop it in your trunk and dispose of the contents at your leisure. Sessions can be held when the toy population, in your paternal opinion, is getting out of control.

Afterward, all you have to do is prepare for interrogation in case your wife or a nosy relative notices something missing.

The Classic Missing Toy Alibi

1. "The dog ate It." (large items)
2. "Baby ate It." (small items)
3. "It broke and I tried to fix It, but..."
4. "You know how Things fall in the garbage disposal sometimes?"
5. "That? I don't remember That."
6. "Check the vacuum cleaner."

[80]

7. "Ask Baby. I'm innocent."

8. "It must have dropped out of the stroller before we left the mall."

9. "Have you looked in the (closet, den, bed room, kitchen)?"

10. "I think we left It at Aunt _____'s."

⌐   ⌐   ⌐   ⌐   ⌐

Toys on Permanent Vacation: the Smart Way Out

If you have doubts about having Baby judge the performance of a given toy, you can always rate them objectively yourself. By the time Baby is ten-months-old, you'll know how easily a person or object can incur violent disfavor depending on his/her prevailing mood.

In fact, after becoming intimate with the average infant's tyrannical nature (see Chapter Six) and bipolar tendencies, you may indeed know his/her judgment to be unreliable. In that case, the following judging method and sample rating chart may be helpful.

Patterned after the formats of human resources departments in major corporations, this totally unbiased rating system is custom-tailored to consider a father's perspective.

[81]

With pen and paper (or on the computer, if you must), in a matter of minutes, you can properly assess and neatly dispose of a dozen poor performers. Serve them the paperwork in person. Make it look like a pink slip with "Permanent Leave of Absence" at the top and your signature at the bottom.

But before you send them packing, please heed this brief caution. Though the grading system has gone through rigorous testing and is certified to be 100% objective, your methodology is best kept under wraps. I wouldn't leave toy pink slips lying around for prying eyes. No need to confuse neighbors or busy-body relatives. The details of your refined technique deserve secure storage...in a locked drawer or accessible only by password within your computer.

Then you can keep toy personnel files right where they need to be. Between you and Baby.

Rating Legend

Performance	Point Value
Outstanding	10
Superior	8
Good	4
Variable	0
Poor	-4
Rotten	-8
The Worst	-10

After examining an item, simply give it a qualitative value for each performance characteristic, then look across the legend on the opposite page and translate your opinion into a precise quantitative measurement.

Check the following traditional candidates and compare them to your experience.

Sample Toy Ratings

(+50)

MORTON SALT BOX

Cost: Outstanding*

Durability: Superior

Safety: Outstanding

Convenience: Outstanding

Educational quality: Variable

Infant Appeal: Good

Dog Appeal: Good

Dad Appeal: Good

Recommendation:

Keep and clone as needed

*free with purchase of salt

(-24)

ROCKING HORSE**

Cost: Variable

Durability: Variable

Safety: Variable

Convenience: The Worst

Educational quality: Poor

Infant Appeal: Good

Dog Appeal: Poor

Dad Appeal: The Worst

Recommendation:

Abandon in unopened box

**boxed; assembly required

[83]

(+8)
STACKABLE BLOCKS
Cost: Variable

Durability: Good

Safety: Variable

Convenience: Rotten

Educational quality: Good

Infant Appeal: Good

Dog Appeal: Superior

Dad Appeal: Poor

Recommendation:

Put on Probation

(+26)
SQUEAKING BUNNY
Cost: Variable

Durability: Variable

Safety: Good

Convenience: Good

Educational quality: Variable

Infant Appeal: Superior

Dog Appeal: Outstanding

Dad Appeal: Variable

Recommendation:

Retain as dog chew

(-10)
DRUM
Cost: Variable

Durability: Poor (with luck)

Safety: Variable

Convenience: Poor

Educational quality: Variable

Infant Appeal: Outstanding

Dog Appeal: Poor

Dad Appeal: Rotten

Recommendation:

Terminate

(+64)
CAR SEAT GADGET*
Cost: Outstanding (no factor)

Durability: Outstanding

Safety: Outstanding

Convenience: Superior

Educational quality: Superior

Infant Appeal: Superior**

Dog Appeal: Variable

Dad Appeal: Outstanding

Recommendation:

Promote

*entertains Baby on long drives
**Holds infant's attention for ten minutes—sometimes longer

A Fond Farewell to Toyland

Naturally, your ratings may differ significantly from the objects on display here. These examples are merely designed to help you become familiar with the system.

Yet, after conducting interviews and assigning the proper numerical value for each career focus, you will possess a perfectly accurate method of comparison. Thus, a rocking horse with required assembly would earn a total value of -24. On the other hand, a quality car seat gadget would be up for promotion with an impressive +64.

Exactly what number should you establish as a benchmark for keepers? Should you, as a resourceful sire, rely on a dividing line that is high, low, or in the middle of the chart?

Well, since you're in charge of the system, I would say that decision is strictly up to you. After all, you're working hard to create a new daddy attitude in a difficult age. Once upon a time you may have been known as a young, opinionated wise-guy. Now you're rapidly growing into the time-honored, enlightened role of a wise paternal leader. Which means you're smart enough now to keep most opinions to yourself.

On the subject of toy terminating, if all else fails, just put your trust in the old saying, *Father Knows Best.* (It may not be true, but it's a nice line to fall back on when your last alibi falls through.)

Chapter six

Infant Tyranny— a Devil of a Dilemma

⌐   ⌐   ⌐   ⌐   ⌐   ⌐   ⌐

Changes, changes, changes. At first glance, especially in the first few months, it will appear to both you and your wife that all you do is spend a lot of time changing Baby (and his/her environment). You change formulas, change diapers, change bed linens, change clothes and on and on and on.

But of course, all the while, what is actually happening is that Baby is changing you.

In its early stages this harmless yet ominous phenomenon forces lightweight lifestyle adjustments. You might even find yourself amused. Later on, the seriousness of the

[87]

situation slaps you. The fascination pales. You're no longer in control. Half the time Baby keeps you rattled, dazed and confused...until, well, you're really not sure what's going on. No need to worry, though. You'll regain your composure again—in another twenty years or so.

Until then, being the father, formerly a dominating force and once the sole object of unlimited family affection, you must face today's cold truth: nothing will ever be the same again.

You used to be Mr. Courageous, *macho-cool-one*, the focus of blind admiration and lusty physical desire. Now you're a ghostly figure floating on the edges of the real scene, a brave but vulnerable character chasing an elusive new identity. You and your love-mate have little time for games of passion. In fact, if you had time to vote on it, both of you would probably settle for an uninterrupted bowel movement every other day.

Meanwhile Baby gets the best of both worlds...unbridled maternal love and a special brand of Daddy-doting anytime he/she strikes a pose. Day after day the routine coasts. You and Mommy scurry and serve, stopping only late at night to sleepily wonder at Baby's growing control of your life.

As the months go by you make a helpless discovery. You've become the victim of a cunning coup, your powers usurped by a little person less than a yard long—a tiny, demanding despot who now calls the shots. Yes, by the time you realize it, it's already too late. You're at the mercy of his/her every whim. The most you can hope for now is an occasional kind word (or sound), a soft glance, affectionate smile or other sign that he/she still respects what you used to be...when things were different.

But let's look at the situation objectively. One could make an argument that we shouldn't go around judging Baby's actions too harshly. For goodness sake, he or she didn't have a choice in the original decision. You were the only slaves on the horizon so he/she is just making do with you.

You never know, maybe Baby would prefer a faster draw on the bottle or a less frequent tweak on the cheek. Or maybe deep-down Baby thinks you should take all of your goo-goo/ga-ga action and stuff it in your nightshirt.

Besides, if you stop and think about it, playing the part of a ruthless dictator has its responsibilities. Even in a small household. And that's a tough assignment when, just because you can't walk well or talk clearly, everyone has this habit of looking down on you.

The news from the front, I'm afraid, keeps getting more confusing instead of less. I couldn't believe it when I heard it. But there's a good deal of new evidence which indicates many children from the age of six- or seven-months to four-years are, in fact, possessed by evil spirits.

⌐   ⌐   ⌐   ⌐   ⌐

I can certainly understand how this information may unsettle or even startle you. I mean, we're talking Exorcist here. And you're already in the middle of making so many adjustments, who needs updates about a dialogue with the man down-under. Just ask Linda Blair's Father.

That's why, at my request, a staff of researchers took the time to uncover several documented Father-Child cases that suggest rather strongly the average infant is simply not in control of his/her actions. Taking it a step further, I compared this revealing data to my own experience and immediately saw remarkable similarities.

You may or may not have the same impression. Devil or angel...you may never fully understand which is witch. But the field reports you're about to read seem to present particularly damning evidence.

At first glance, after a quick read-through, you might put each of the following case histories in the same camp as the tabloids you try not to look at in the supermarket checkout lane. The difference is, these documented accounts trade alien UFOs and bizarre cults for everyday tots in babeland. The two reports which follow may seem far-fetched but they hit close to home.

What possesses these little people to do the things they do? Who the devil can explain it?

Keep and open mind and read on, Papa-san. Only then can you make an intelligent, honorable conclusion.

CASE HISTORY NO. 1
The Cannibalistic Surprise

Fred Stuman, accountant, arrived home after a hard day's work and long commute from the city. He kissed his wife and nine-month-old daughter, fixed himself a drink, then sat down in the den to relax and read the evening paper.

Fred knew his daughter had been teething lately. This was the main reason, he supposed, for her bad mood the day before. Yesterday, she had been cranky and crying, drooling excessively and unwilling to eat.

But tonight Trish seemed in fine spirits as she happily crawled from room to room, babbling inquisitively, exploring every household artifact in sight. After a while, Fred put aside the stress of his corporate workday and sought Trish for a little old-fashioned father-infant entertainment. Actually what Fred had in mind was a toned-down game of "Horsey."

A little tired, he could have easily opted for a less aerobic activity. But around this house, especially before bedtime bottle, Horsey absolutely reigned as the infant sport of choice. No matter how many times they played it every week.

So Fred bounced little Trish on his knee, tentatively at first, then faster and faster, listening to her timid giggles turn to wild squeals. She obviously enjoyed having time with her father.

Between bounces Fred started thinking about Trish's teething pains and wondered if she had a new tooth to go with a trio fully grown-in, it seemed, for weeks now.

"Let me see those toothies," he said, tickling her until she laughed even harder, mouth open wide. Fred looked inside.

Fred tickled. Trish laughed and laughed. Then lunging forward, without warning—except for a malevolent flash in her eyes—Trish snatched Fred's glasses, screamed, and bit him viciously on the nose.

Fred screamed and Trish screamed and Mommy screamed (when she saw Fred's nose) and Fred cursed and Trish laughed and Mommy cried and they never played Horsey again.

Why?

CASE HISTORY NO. 2
The Gangplank Ritual

Little Billy, eleven-months, acted very strangely at times and his parents, Mr. and Mrs. Black, couldn't understand it. A mild-mannered little tyke in ordinary situations, Billy had begun to develop a bizarre relationship with many of his favorite toys.

[92]

His mother, Belinda, noticed it first and informed Billy's father. "You should see what he did to his monkey today," she said. Then she told him about a gutted cat-in-the-hat doll, a mutilated clown and an unstuffed doggie.

"But he only does it when he's in his crib or playpen, above the ground."

"What?" Roger replied, "Come on—you're imagining things."

Roger, a jolly, bearded fellow, took care of Billy every other weekend when Belinda worked an early shift at the hospital. One Saturday morning he was awakened by loud noises coming from the baby's room.

"What the hell is that," he muttered, half asleep, stumbling down the hall. As he got closer, the noises got louder and louder, and Roger realized it was some sort of shouting, or perhaps bellowing. He turned the doorknob and heard a kind of brutish bark, sounding somehow like a command.

Mr. Black opened the door slightly and peered in.

There was Billy standing at the crib railing looking down at a pile of toys on the floor. Roger watched as Billy bent over and gently picked up a little teddy beside his pillow. It was the last toy left in the crib. He looked at it for a second and began babbling, softly at first, then louder.

Briefly he thrust the bear's face through the safety railing of the crib, squashed snout painfully plump between the wooden bars, button-eyes wide and slightly crossed. Billy looked at the back of the furry head and addressed it with a peculiar half-growl. Carefully he clutched the teddy by the arm and moved it to the top of the railing.

For a long moment Billy babbled quietly to himself, balancing the bear on top of the crib rail overlooking a sea of plush companions scattered about the carpeted floor. Suddenly he turned the bear around, shouting fiercely in its face, savagely flinging the animal over the side onto the pile.

Mr. Black pushed open the bedroom door and tiptoed in. "Son?" he said, anxiously.

Billy surveyed his crib mates on the floor and grunted with satisfaction. Then he looked up at his father and smiled like an angel.

Why?

⌐   ⌐   ⌐   ⌐   ⌐

As Cute as the Devil?

Alarming? Absolutely. Unusual? Hardly. The worst misfortune about the preceding evidence is that it is all too typical. Keep in mind that these encounters add up to one pair out of dozens and dozens of verified incidents.

There are cases on record of normal infants suddenly lapsing into uncontrollable tantrums in the tub. Even more of usually well-behaved babies erupting in their high chairs, splattering food all over their unsuspecting parents. Many cases report the cruel treatment of pets, including dog ear-pulling, tail-twisting and more.

Are these indications of a demon-driven little lamb that deserves your compassion and understanding? Are there voices in Baby's head telling him/her what to do? Or is this a wolf in sheep's clothing, a deceptive little tyrant merely trying to pull the wool over your eyes?

It could be that all babies (as well as toddlers) are simply manic-depressive types, yet modern research hasn't discovered it. Perhaps the contemporary term, bipolar disorder, makes more sense in describing the infant population's legendary mood swings.

Whatever the cause of an infant's autocratic and/or erratic behavior, it's a dilemma every father must deal with sooner or later. It's true whether your child assumes the role of a wild-eyed schizophrenic or simply a cool-headed, efficient schemer.

You might decide to delay this tormenting assessment for months. When it first happens to them, few fathers are willing to admit that Baby is a bewildering gyroscope, either A) spinning along, perfectly oscillated or B) flopping upside-down, tangled and twitching, totally out-of-whack.

Either admission proves once and for all that big, bad Dad is the one who has lost control of the situation. Some Daddies become so intimidated they even try to ignore the problem. Somehow they get their pre-Pop and post-Pop identities mixed up. They refuse to recognize that relics of the ancient, pre-Pop world apply evermore only in a father's professional life.

No matter. Quickly comes the day when all of us must choose a course of action. Which way should you go?

Institute a get-tough policy with suitable punishment for frequent offenders? Appeal to Baby's sense of fairness, pleading with him/her to see the light and do the right thing? Or how about outright bribery as a persuasive tool?

The biggest danger lies in becoming irrational, losing your temper—doing something a mature father regrets. Baby will only seek revenge later and make you pay doubly for your arrogance. So try not to show anger. And do your best to keep upset feelings below the surface. Hostilities have to be put in check, even if the temptation (in the heat of battle) seems more than you can possibly bear.

Take heart in knowing that many abused fathers are finally coming out of the closet, telling the truth, exorcising their feelings of shame and guilt. You may also find some helpful hints in Chapter Eight, *Secrets to Avoiding Infant Abuse.*

Unfortunately, no matter how carefully you prepare, there are few easy answers at the end of a nerve-shattering afternoon when your patience is spent, the computer crashes, the repairman knocks, the kettle boils over and Baby decides to put a broomstick up the cat's behind.

Chapter seven

Day Care
Litters
and Baby Sitter
Jitters

⌐   ⌐   ⌐   ⌐   ⌐   ⌐   ⌐

The amazing thing about taking care of infants
is that you have even more to worry about
when you're not taking care of them

It's not just the reputation of mothers in general. You know the truth from years of subliminal research listening to your own mom: *mothers have refined the art of worrying into an exact science.* The very moment your wife gives birth she will instinctively begin worrying. Forever after she will be blessed

[99]

with the ability to worry so efficiently that you'll never actually know how well she does it. You might think you know, but you won't. The infinite range and profound genius of our wives' worrying power are really light years beyond our comprehension.

The first-time father, on the opposite end of the parental solar system, is a pitifully undisciplined worrier. Depending on your personality, it could take you months to learn to worry more decisively. Don't despair, though, your offspring is remarkably adept at helping you to learn as quickly as possible.

Learning to Worry with Precision

You begin by thinking about Baby's impending medical problems. Your imagination welcomes everyday evils and exotic diseases with equal cheer. Start with ordinary jaundice and chronic colic, then move on to retroactive diaper rash, creeping black lung, carpal tunnel syndrome, small pox, scurvy, delirium tremens, bubonic plague, swine flu fever and Amazonian jungle rot.

Soon health worries are buoyed by abstract parental concerns...troubles that come to the surface only in the complex context of our happy-go-lucky adult world. Joyless things like supplemental health insurance, permanent disability, unfunded retirement funds, short-term employment, long-term debt, stock market drops, family-planning flops, and finally, a suitable plot for old belly-up Pops.

Before long the onset of acute mental and physical disorders will let you know that you have graduated to worrying on a higher plane.

Fixation on Baby's likely health problems gives you a case of perpetual indigestion, the result of promiscuous ulcers dancing all around your stomach lining. You walk around jiggling internally, strange forces doing the rumba in your tummy, eyelids fluttering, looking for your offspring's latest signs of illness.

Hypothetical worries about Baby's future spark a host of nerve-related health issues any hypochondriac would be proud to own. You see the first signs as irreversible facial-twitching (especially eyelids and upper lip), the sure result of growing brain tumors. In your mind you brace yourself for attacks of erectile dysfunction, foot drop and raging flatulence quick to follow.

At any juncture if you slip back into your old ways and forget to worry yourself silly for a few minutes, all you have to think about is this:

the cost of your son's/daughter's college education will likely be ten times what it costs today.

There! Back on track?

[101]

All of the above, taken as a whole, serves to help you worry more. And that's the price we men pay for not having learned to worry earlier in life when our mothers told us to.

⌐   ⌐   ⌐   ⌐   ⌐

Hard Work Made Easy: Child Care Choices for Career Parents

Talk about worries. If male pattern baldness hasn't claimed you yet, the anxiety of major child care decisions will make you slick with worry in a hurry. Institutional day care? Move-in-Nanny? Mother-in-Law on permanent loan? The fallout from any and all of these decisions will be agonizing. Day by day you and your spouse make the choices. Strand by strand your hair becomes history. Either way, you can count on getting the shaft.

Unless you happen to be independently wealthy (of your wife, that is) the care your infant receives when the two of you are working becomes a primary concern. Even if you run a home office, you'll never get anything done running around looking after (or for) your offspring.

Even if your wife is a proud stay-at-home mom, she (more than anyone) could use an occasional break. Even if you run a cash-cow Internet site with a bank of servers in your basement, sooner or later, you will still encounter the tangled web of child care.

Only if you're wealthy enough to afford an au pair will you not need much of the following advice. Au pair's bring their own set of problems...too many to go into in this simple book.

Yes, choosing child care can be a big, bad stress-builder. But as full-time workers and loving parental units, at least your options are clearly defined.

You and your spouse can:

(1) Make the popular choice and decide to enroll Baby in the best day care center you can afford

(2) Invite your mother-in-law to move in with you on a permanent basis

(3) Hire a professional day-nanny to come to your home

(4) Find a smart person in your neighborhood who has quit his/her regular job to start a lucrative stay-at-home child care business

Option One: The Day Care Center

Quicker than a greasy burger off a franchise grill, the neighborhood day care facility has spread itself all over the face of suburbia. Even in the city it's taken the place of the once revered corner gas station (with a real garage, full-service pumps but no feminine hygiene products or low-fat frozen entrees) as an authentic American landmark. In other words, no matter where you live, you shouldn't have a problem finding a day care operation.

In fact, you'll probably have a choice. So here are a few tips you may want to keep in mind during your first inspection tour:

As you drive into the garage or parking lot, you'll pass the fenced-in "play area" (where there used to be grass) and you'll know you're at the right place. Walk into the reception area and wait for someone to greet you. Be patient—the sights, sounds and smells should convince you that people here are very busy. Since you have a particular interest in the infant-care area, ask the representative to show it to you and Mommy. No need to ask where it is; you'll know you're getting close when its distinctive fragrance reaches you.

Upon entering the infant zone, don't be alarmed if you suddenly feel a dozen pairs of little eyes staring at you—as if you're some giant alien from the planet Zargrob. This is normal. After all, you are strange (and rather large) intruders into their daily routine. At this time you may want to ask yourself a few questions as you develop a general impression of the place and its personnel.

For example, are the cribs lined up neatly in formation, like well-kept cages in a good zoo? Is the floor clean? Does the person in charge of the infants seem to have a reasonable intelligence? What percentage of snotty noses are there in the crowd? Does the overall scene remind you subconsciously of the dog kennel down the street?

These and other factors should be honestly appraised. Only then can you and your wife make a responsible decision.

Concerning Day Care Costs:

As a paternal figure, you may find the day care center to be an attractive option depending on local competition. But don't expect too much. Unlike your favorite fast food franchise, day care chains don't ordinarily offer web site discounts, value menus, 2-for-1 specials or drive-through windows. Yet.

Option Two:
The Move-in Mother-in-Law

Before you seriously contemplate this lunatic act, I suggest you look around the house for things to sell. We've all been short on cash before, but believe me, you can work through this.

At least find an item to pawn that will buy enough time for you to think the matter over. A second job could be the answer. Or perhaps a well-planned bank robbery. Just put your imagination to work and leave this cruel fate to those embarrassing fictitious papas in cable sitcoms.

Option Three: The Day-Nanny

The day-nanny is a person who arrives at your doorstep five mornings a week and spends the day caring for your infant in your own home. Then in the evening, after a parent takes control, the day-nanny generally leaves under his/her own power. This is certainly convenient. It is also extremely expensive. But not nearly as expensive as a true live-in nanny.

With this latter brand of nanny, you might be required to provide, in addition to a handsome salary: three meals a day, free laundry, furnished living quarters and nightly entertainment. This could give you the feeling you've added two new family members instead of one. Besides, if you could afford a nanny like that, odds are you wouldn't be reading this chapter in the first place. You'd have an au pair instead.

Ultimately, even for well-to-do dads, the tax complications alone are enough to squash the concept of full-time help. In the long term, part-time caretakers might just make more sense for less cents.

Another advantage of hiring a day-nanny is that you don't have to remove Baby from his/her normal environment. Of course while you and your wife are away all day earning a living, Nanny may be removing objects other than Baby from Baby's environment. Such as jewelry, camera equipment, computer peripherals and/or your good china.

That's why it is wise to select day-nannies through a dependable referral service.

Option Four: Private Day Care

Private day care, as opposed to commercial day care, means an unlicensed, non-franchised individual (not to be confused with disenfranchised) taking children into his or her home daily for fun and profit. Mostly profit.

By state law, there is generally a limit to the number of children one person may care for at a time, depending also on the size of the residence. The care giver-to-child ratio should be relatively low—five to one, for instance. You can promptly see what a positive aspect this might bring to Baby's environment. Logically speaking, he/she should receive more individual attention than that offered in a large, commercial center.

To illustrate, however, that the notion about "individual" attention may be misleading, all you have to do is imagine yourself caring for Baby every day, five days a week. Just you and Baby. Then multiply by another five.

Through simple mathematics you can get the real lowdown on why these child care entrepreneurs charge higher fees than you might guess. Sure, they're making big bucks now. But like a running back in pro football, they can only play the game for a relatively short time. Then the bruises, bumps and mental anguish force them into an early retirement.

Like a scatback, private day care entrepreneurs are also hard to catch. But don't let that stop you if you've decided to pursue one. Next are a few hints which may help lead you to a proper selection among potential candidates. Just remember. If you like one based on these signs, don't let him/her get away.

[107]

The Private Day Care
Personal Interview...

Apply these quick tips to your initial interview session and note the good (and not-so-good) aspects of your first impressions:

It's a GOOD SIGN if the care giver's home is tidy, comfortable and unassuming.

It could be a BAD SIGN if the care giver has plastic covers on the furniture, runners on the rugs, a copy of *Mommy Dearest* on the coffee table and tells you to take off your shoes and wash your hands before entering the living room.

It's certainly a GOOD SIGN if the care giver's own children are happy and well-behaved.

It might be a BAD SIGN if the care giver starts showing off a large collection of ceramic ashtrays made by his/her teenage son in the state penitentiary.

It's always a GOOD SIGN if the care giver appears to be sober, humble and serious about his/her work.

It may be a BAD SIGN if, during your morning interview, the care giver hands you a bloody mary and asks if you'd like to smoke a couple of doobies.

It's a definite GOOD SIGN if the care giver generously provides toys as well as comfort items, including play pens and cribs for the children's use.

It's probably a BAD SIGN if you walk into a children's play area furnished exclusively with ropes, whips, chains and assorted padlocks.

It might be a GOOD SIGN if the care giver lives in a well-established, safe-looking neighborhood.

It's most likely a BAD SIGN if the area features a lot of neon signage, abandoned cars, barbed wire fence tops and nervous attack dogs.

It's a sure GOOD SIGN if the care giver avoids discussions of politics and religious beliefs.

It's often a BAD SIGN if there are pictures of Adolf Hitler on the wall and the care giver is wearing a white sheet with dragons and swastikas embroidered on it.

Tender Is the Nighttime Sitter

After months of virtual solitary confinement, you and your wife will one day feel the impulse to break out, get crazy, go wild—just the two of you—alone. That's when you plan a madcap evening of cocktails and dinner at your favorite restaurant. The radically adventurous may even try to see a current movie at a first-run theater.

So who do you get to look after Baby on your big night out? A specialist, of course. In this field of scarce, highly-paid, demanding experts, the candidates happen to be innocent, easily distracted adolescent females, age 13 to 19. Exactly the type of prey you pursued so feverishly when you were their age. No matter whose house you had to pursue them in.

Remember?

Well, nothing has changed. Neither rain nor snow nor gloom of night will prevent babysitters' boyfriends from making their appointed rounds. It's too bad if that makes you feel uneasy—you should have thought about that a long time ago.

One way you might attempt to solve this problem is to somehow locate a sitter who positively doesn't have a current boyfriend. Or a prospective one.

What you're looking for is either:

(a) a girl with a halo
  or
(b) a female version of the elephant man

Good luck. If you find either caliber of young lady, you can consider yourself a fortunate man indeed.

Undoubtedly, a more practical solution is to beef up the security around your home.

When your sitter is alone in your house, think of her as Cinderella in a castle under siege. It might help if you could dig a moat around the house and barricade every door and window. But this solution could be exceedingly expensive and your neighbors might object. You could always hire a thug with a club to hide in the bushes and beat the young men away from the front door. But that remedy might lead to lawsuits. Very costly, start to finish.

No, the only reasonable precaution is to place electronic security devices at every possible point of entry. Don't neglect second-story windows and chimneys if you have them.

Be fair and warn your sitter of these important preparations. Tell her your brand of Homeland Security is solely for her protection. Also tell her that any loud music, any door or window opening, any extended telephone conversation will set off a series of devastating air raid sirens followed, in seconds, by the arrival of the local police escorted by a special contingent of off-duty vice squad investigators.

Along with a few CIA-style wiretaps and hidden microphones, these wise safeguards should give you peace of mind on your night out. On the other hand, after watching you wire the back door with computer-monitored electroshock sensors, your wife will probably stare at you for a long time and shake her head.

Then she'll most likely raise her eyebrows and say something like this: "Well, Daddy-O. It looks like you've really lost your marbles this time. What will Baby and the neighbors think?"

That's when you suddenly feel your ulcers on the prowl and your nerves crackling across synapse all through your body. Yet you smile (like a fox, lip twitching) and say,

"You might be right, Dear. This whole sitter episode is beginning to make me...well, just a little bit unsteady. I don't *really* feel crazy (eyes wide and frozen) but maybe—just maybe—my mind is beginning to slip.

"Still, there's one thing I know for sure. I'm not as young as I used to be, that's true. But I haven't lost my memory yet, thank you very much."

Safe at Home,
Parents' Night Out

Chapter eight

Secrets to Avoiding Infant Abuse

⌐   ⌐   ⌐   ⌐   ⌐   ⌐   ⌐

How do you escape being abused by an infant? It might be helpful if you were an invisible man or the inventor of a portable cloaking device similar to the one used on *Star Trek*. But since these intriguing fantasies exist only in bad movies and science fiction syndication, we have to look for other ways to outwit the normal infant's sadistic tendencies.

You may occasionally hear a discussion (at the supermarket or in your analyst's office) about "good babies" versus "bad babies" and opinions about each. When you and Baby are out together shopping, someone might even walk up to you

[113]

in the checkout line and say, "My, what a good baby you have. What a little angel! You sure are lucky."

But when you get home with Baby, and it's just the two of you with an empty afternoon ahead, you know in your heart that there are no good babies. There are also no "angel" babies and no "lucky" babies. There are only bad babies and worse babies.

Of course, even a rotten infant has his/her good moments. These you should cherish. And while you're cherishing them, start thinking about what to do when this blissful reprieve is over.

First, you need to learn how to recognize when your child has abuse on his/her mind. Watch Baby closely and you will see the signs. Brows become furrowed, lips press together tightly, pupils contract and his/her chin stiffens into little crinkles. When you see this happening, you have just a split-second to react. You are about to be bopped over the head, spit on, kicked in the stomach or screamed at. Now is the time to nip this abuse in the bud. You must act quickly, utilizing the latest techniques in time-snitching, daddy-style distraction.

Techniques of distraction are fundamental and effective as a weapon in combating infant-daddy attacks. As a bonus, distraction can be almost undetectable, like a Stealth fighter brushing the treetops, sneaking in low under Baby's radar screen. The key is staying armed and alert, knowing when to pull the trigger.

[114]

Be warned. As powerful as distraction may be, all the distraction power in the world sometimes fails. You'll understand soon enough. Baby is brilliant at this business of abuse.

Dodging Abuse through Distraction

Turn the infant's short attention span to your advantage. Engage him/her in a stimulating new activity. If your timing is right, Baby will instantly forget what he/she wanted to do to you. After all, infants are very spontaneous people. They're just out for a good time. Naturally it gives them extra pleasure if the fun is at your expense. Being an informed paternal figure, you should be aware that nothing appeals to Baby's sense of humor quite like seeing his/her big, strong father writhing in pain from a well-placed finger poke.

In a recent poll, surviving father-caretakers were asked how they went about escaping this kind of unprovoked assault. The results of these essay questions present an insider's look at modern tactics of infant distraction actually used in the field. Thanks to the generous advice of these trailblazing veterans, stumbling tenderfoots like you and me still have a sporting chance.

(1) Learning to be a Smart Gamekeeper

Even the wildest infant can be partially controlled through a well-stocked repertoire of traditional baby games. Although old-fashioned, absurdly simple and undignified, these little activities can be most dependable allies in managing abuse. Like pork and beans over a campfire, they're not gourmet quality—just satisfying. That's why you'll find a generous helping in Chapter Eleven (*Fun and Games for Fathers and Other Fools*). You're sure to discover two or three that have special meaning for your infant's uniquely twisted psychological makeup.

Then when Baby has you cornered on the couch with an ugly look of aggression on his/her face, you can whip out your trusty Peek-A-Boo routine and exhibit true grace under pressure.

(2) Driving Baby to Distraction

Without exception, every father-caretaker interrogated placed this category high on his list. One father wrote, "I'll always remember fondly the hours we spent rolling down the interstate in air-conditioned comfort, soft jazz on the stereo, Baby sleeping peacefully in the rear view mirror."

Another veteran said, "Take my advice—thank the man who invented the wheel. When things got rough, I used to throw Jimbo in a snuggle sack, strap him to my back and hop on a bike. We'd ride around the neighborhood, happy as clams."

The moral is, before infants discover self-propelled locomotion to be a reliable alternative, they have a definite weakness for most any set of wheels. You can put them in a stroller, wagon, scooter, bus, semi-truck, train, tractor or wheelbarrow. Most babies don't care as long as you don't stop.

They just want to GO-GO-GO. So make the most of this strategy while you can. When infants learn to crawl—then walk—they want to do all the going themselves. You'll never again trap Baby with his/her blessing for more than a few minutes.

Worse still, thanks to the passage of painful yet necessary car seat-restraint laws, you won't know the pleasure of long-distance automobile travel for many years. Making sounds like a dying camel, your buckled-up offspring will stretch dreamy, picture-postcard miles into an endless desert of the damned. Into the night, without joy or hope you will suffer the reality of your progeny's woe. Every crack in the pavement will be a crater. Every pair of headlights kissing your bumper will be a speeding tractor-trailer. Every shriek from the back seat will mock your pitiful New Age CD.

Supermarket Cart: Rare Wheels that Just Won't Work

(3) Washing Your Troubles Away

A warm, relaxing bath can be a special event for both father and child. Of course, you don't have to get in the tub if you don't want to. There may not be enough room for the two of you, anyway. Plus Baby may decide not to share his/her favorite tub toys. This would create more tension, turning a pleasant interlude into an unnecessary confrontation.

As far as baths and abuse are concerned, the most important guideline to observe is to undress your infant speedily. If you're slow at this stage, his/her small burst of violence could escalate into full-blown rage. The last thing you need is a bathroom riot on your hands...some sort of violent soap opera with a teary ending.

Being fast, however, doesn't mean you should rip Baby's clothes off and throw him/her in the water like an anchor from the *Good Ship Lollipop*. Baths without drownings are much more fun for all concerned. Just try to be quick or look for an easier distraction. A bath isn't the answer for every father or every brooding infant.

You might consider a quick shower if a dip in the tub conjures images of bubble baths and femininity and makes you feel uncomfortable. However, this is recommended only with mobile infants of twenty pounds or more, babies you don't have to lift and place like a wobbly bowling pin at the end of the alley. Otherwise images of slippery, dropped balls and sickening thuds may spoil the mood entirely.

(4) Promoting Yourself as a "Pop" Singer

The charms of a sweet lullaby have been used by mothers for centuries to trick uncooperative infants into a respite of blessed sleep. Dairy farmers pipe music into milking parlors to cajole contented guernseys into increased production. Major corporations use the same theory to keep their herds happy. So it should be no secret that music can help you reduce abuse.

Yet many male parents fail to recognize its power—though a well-phrased melody can practically halt a charging infant in his/her tracks.

The men in our survey indicated an emerging, albeit reluctant awareness of music's potential. Even these cagey, dogfaced veterans of infant combat seemed to be afraid to try it. As if singing to an infant could somehow be embarrassing. Who's going to complain? Baby can't even talk, much less criticize your voice or choice of material.

Pride is the culprit here. Fathers who act like musical scaredy-cats simply let the pride of their former personality creep back in the picture. Standing around talking about pride with oatmeal-encrusted eyebrows just doesn't make sense. Think about it. The sooner you get in tune with today's reality, the better.

Truthfully, between you and me, a singing poppa does have the edge here. But don't despair if you can't carry a tune. Even a tone-deaf dud of a dad can be a good hummer.

[119]

Besides, there are radios, compact discs, DVDs and multimedia computers at your disposal. In addition, you'll be glad to know that the common offspring has an incredibly eclectic musical taste.

Infants and toddlers have been known to appreciate such diverse artists as George Gershwin, Julio Iglesias and The Grateful Dead. In a two-hour span, Baby may swing from Big Band to Classical to Rhythm & Blues. All you need to remember is match the music to the mood. If Baby looks ready for a destructive rampage, turn on some loud Beethoven. Get him/her involved. If he/she seems a little hysterical, slightly out-of-touch—slip a Jimi Hendrix CD in the machine and go with the flow. The important thing is to keep the platters spinning...and the audience grinning.

The really inventive dad might decide to throw in a disc jockey impersonation just to keep things lively. Holding a rattle as a microphone, you could introduce each tune. But beware, some babies may balk at this degree of heavy-handed showmanship, so use discretion along with your imagination. The point is, by making music your ally against abuse, you can keep Baby off-balance (and harmonious) for hours on end.

(For a collection of musical hints to match the mood of the moment, please refer to the brief *Music Bibliography* at the back of the book.)

(5) Turning Abuse Inside/Out

This sure cure for the baby blues is a fail-safe inspiration, weather permitting. Let's say you and your short-fused babe are trapped together for the entire weekend because Mom is attending an out-of-town seminar. By Sunday afternoon, you and the newest family member have played games, taken rides, baths and about as much music as you can stand. You're developing a severe case of cabin fever. The mirror reveals a gaunt, hunted look—as your crawling ten-month-old stalks you from room to room.

You need a new trick...a magic potion or pinch of daddy wizardry to induce a brighter spell.

Well, the happy ending to this gloomy scenario is clear. Just grab Baby as quickly as possible and get outside. Take a walk. Tour the neighborhood. Better yet, find a nice green park nearby. Every infant loves the great outdoors. You would too if you had recently been stuffed in a small, dark cave for forty weeks...a place where the sole menu listed daily specials of semi-digested leftovers served up through your belly-button. Talk about a raw deal in solitary confinement.

Think about the freedom of outdoor living from Baby's viewpoint. A tranquil park. Quiet pathways bordered by shady trees. A perfect spot in the center of a sloping meadow with a great dome of a sky overhead. Giant shadows bending over your blanket blocking the sun. Bad adult breath and ridiculous cooing sounds. An uninvited, tender index finger ripe for biting.

Off the blanket, new and exotic things to touch, smell, see, hear, and most of all, eat.

More than anything, babies love to put foreign objects in their mouths. Every substance in the universe, liquid or

[121]

solid, must pass your infant's taste test. This is mandatory. It can also be a disgusting experience in popular city parks with no dog-walking paths. So take care when you take a rest and place Baby near natural turf. Otherwise your lighthearted outdoor scene might lapse into stomach-turning melodrama.

Besides doggie deposits, there could be poisonous weeds, harmful flowers, unhealthy chemicals, garbage, broken glass and other injurious materials in any natural setting. Moreover, there are always crawling things hiding in the clover with names that you and I can't pronounce. Even a semi-mobile infant will discover several of these creatures and eat them whole within seconds.

Indoors or out, nothing can stop Baby from exploring his or her surroundings. After a wicked bee sting or chunky burp-up from munching wildflowers, he/she may long for the fun times inside Mommy's tummy. Truth be known, in our weak moments when the world seems cruel, it's a place we men fondly recall. But once out and about, as a famous author once noted, you can never go home again.

Good thing this guide is about Baby's problems, not ours. You and your precious small person should get out as often as possible and have a good time. You can come back home anytime.

Just remember, when the two of you find yourselves out discovering nature, it's your job to keep a sharp lookout. As a brave father/protector (and possible cub scout graduate), you should be prepared to meet all the dangers of the great outdoors.

Unfortunately, during the winter season, no parent will ever be prepared for being stuck indoors with a dangerous infant until springtime. I'm afraid that's another in a long line of cold truths. Here's another:

The Truth about Infants and TV

By the time your offspring reaches the cynical age of eight or nine months, he/she will have become much too blasé about TV programming for it to have any breathtaking distraction value. True, Baby may appreciate *Sesame Street* and an occasional cartoon. But there is little chance, I'm sure you'll agree, of an enraged infant being instantly calmed by a few mild-mannered puppets teaching alphabet phonetics.

The Curse of the Screaming Meemie

It only takes one encounter with this form of abuse to respect the dark art of torture as practiced by ancient infants, passed though the ages to today's sorcerer-tots of the new millennium. A well-versed Screaming Meemie baby inflicts pain so intense the average father will drop to his knees and grovel on the carpet upon hearing the first note. These caustic, raw-pitched wailings have been known to crack plaster and kill parakeets within a twenty-yard radius.

Personally, I would prefer bamboo shoots under my nails or having my beard trimmed with a buzz saw rather than listen to a Screaming Meemie in full command of his/her voice.

[123]

If your infant suddenly exhibits this bloodcurdling trait, the only thing you can do is buy a pair of earplugs and pray for the punishment to be swift. Also—in this situation only—any form of bribery is acceptable. Offer chocolate cookies, pre-sweetened cereal, Flossie's catnip or the all-time ultimate equalizer—*The Bottle*. As a last resort, you may consider hitting the bottle yourself. However, that is not recommended as a long-term solution.

Almost as bad as the Screaming Meemie, though more subtle, are the nauseating sounds of the Sniveling Wimp. This miserable character creates a series of mournful whines accompanied by continuous sniffling and slobbering. The Sniveling Wimp-child transforms ordinary weeping into a marathon event. Hour after hour the insidious whining persists in an anguished sing-song pattern.

The sounds of blubbering float through the air in endless spirals without variation. The sniveler only stops to emphasize his/her pitiful unhappiness by clutching at parents' pant-legs or skirts whenever available. This can result in significant hair-loss for dads who like to wear shorts in the summertime.

After an initial rush of compassion, the average plucked daddy will experience an overpowering urge to park this clinging wretch in a diaper pail and nail the lid. Be strong and resist this temptation. If all else fails, drag clamped-on Baby to the nearest phone and dial the universal AFA (Abused Fathers Anonymous) Hotline:

1-666-NXS-PAIN

[124]

Chapter nine

First Steps/ First Words: The Leaning Tower of Babble

⌐   ⌐   ⌐   ⌐   ⌐   ⌐   ⌐

Learning to walk is literally Baby's first step in establishing independence from his/her lovingly overprotective parents. By the time this triumph is noted in the obligatory pink or blue Baby Book, your infant will be fed up with your ever-watchful worrying and smothering presence. How would you like it if your every movement was captured on film and recorded in an intimate diary for everyone to read?

So you see, infants learn to walk simply because they'd like to get away from you and have a little privacy for a change. Oh yes, by the age of ten months, Baby is also convinced that he/she is on some kind of desperate mission to explore the planet. With only you and Mom *standing* in the way.

On the Brink of Disaster

Baby's crawling days are numbered when he/she pulls to an upright position for the first time. Infants typically use a chair (or parent) leg for this purpose. Suddenly two feet taller, your offspring is delighted with the discovery that his/her mother and father are shrinking. Baby thinks, "They're not such big shots after all. I'll just give them the slip the next time they start popping those electronic flashes in my face."

This historic occasion is indeed followed by weeks of slips and slides, of cruising around the coffee table and lurching from one piece of furniture to the next. Watching in horror, you imagine your little one tumbling head first into the fireplace or smashing his/her skull on the sharp, fluted trim of maw-maw's antique cedar chest. Overnight you're convinced your home has become an infant deathtrap.

In a frenzied rush to redeem your dwelling, you ask yourselves, how can we protect this reckless little prowler? What type of rubber safety net can be constructed? How do you help your stumbling babykins avoid meeting disaster head-on?

First of all, there is no need for panic. Infants are designed to be remarkably hardheaded (except for that strange, porpoise-like softspot on the top). By the time your child reaches full toddlerhood you will know what true hardheaded-ness is all about. Until then, the best thing you can do is to stay in good physical condition yourself.

While Baby is learning to walk, the concerned father will undertake athletic rescue attempts that would test the skills of an Olympic medalist: leaping hurdles across cocktail tables, pinpoint dashes through toy-cluttered kitchens, standing broad jumps over ottomans.

These track & field events may jolt a person's cardio-vascular system, yet they're easy compared to the hours you'll spend standing in the middle of the living room, spine bent, arms outstretched, like a failing weightlifter who just suffered a hernia doing the clean-and-jerk. Saying sweetly, "Come to Da-Da, little girl/boy. You can do it. Just three more steps before Daddy's back breaks. Please."

Once Baby has mastered the art of putting one foot ahead of the other, he/she still has to deal with the difficult question of balance. Sporting tuned-up motor skills and a high-octane energy level, your offspring unfortunately has the equilibrium and judgment of a drunk driver. Now—especially now—it's important to keep your eyes open, steer Baby in the right direction and soften the inevitable collisions when possible.

All in all, it's a staggering responsibility, but you have to stay sober, alert, quick of feet and quick of mind. Do this and you'll soon be through the awkward shuffle-and-flop stage with few disasters—and very little body damage.

On the Road to Discovery

Unmatched in history by dedicated, fearless adult explorers of the highest order, the common baby makes Christopher Columbus look like an uninspired landlubber. The only trouble is...your infant sets sail in every direction at once. And his/her already unsteady course is continuously altered by the most enticing discoveries. A tiny bug in the rug, a minute piece of lint from the washing machine, the exciting LED twinkles from your stereo and CD player...the soft, push-able keys of your unattended cel phone.

All of these revelations coupled with his/her new-found locomotion, get some babies so keyed up they develop a terrible case of infant insomnia—exactly when you'd think the fatigue of exploration would take its toll. After all, *you're* tired.

This affliction can make naptime a rude awakening for parent and child. The naive father, particularly, who expects Baby to cooperate for two hours while he putters happily in the garden is courting bitter disillusionment.

Stuck behind bars in a lonely crib, the just-walking infant regards this as nothing more than a prison sentence. As temporary jailer, you should wise up and forget about personal plans and/or stimulating leisure pursuits. Your job is to keep the prisoner in-line and on-schedule till Head Warden Mommy returns. Insomniac attack or not.

So what can a Daddy do? Wouldn't it be nice to have the calming power of a Mommy-lullaby at your disposal, any-time you needed it. The sure, gentle sight and sweet-flowing sounds of authentic maternal love—instead of your gruff, hairy, good-intentioned fumbling.

What about that sleek, shiny DVD player of yours with its seductive lights and clicking buttons. And the digital movie camera that goes with it. Baby might just sleep like a baby in front of a homemade, dream-inducing video starring Mommy Love, world famous lullaby artist. Get the picture?

⌐   ⌐   ⌐   ⌐   ⌐

The Alien Invasion

Along about the time your incurably curious offspring sets out to explore our planet, you will begin to question whether or not he/she may have somehow come from a different one. Or at minimum, from a terribly foreign country.

Listen closely to the exotic sounds emanating from his/her little mouth. What many non-parents mistake for meaningless babble really has a fluent quality about it. And everything seems to make perfect sense to Baby. Well then, where on earth (we hope) did he/she learn this mysterious language? Who taught it?

[129]

I knew a Californian couple once whose first son was born on an air base in Germany. Little Eric began chattering nonstop a year later, back in Bakersfield. The boy's father, a colonel, along with all of his neighbors, were shocked to detect whole verbs and nouns, amid the clutter, sounds for all the world like some kind of Teutonic dialect. The poor colonel was convinced that someone had made a mistake and switched babies at the hospital.

"The little guy sounds so much like this baker who had a shop near the base," he said, "I'm beginning to think he looks like him, too."

At the time, the only thing I could think of to say was, "Did your wife shop there often?" That was, of course, before I became a father and understood the sort of talk he was talking about.

One has to wonder why stories like the colonel's seem to make no sense at all. And neither do the infant dialects we find ourselves listening to. Can all of it be merely a jumble of jive talk? Or are babies secretly communicating with each other through a special coded jargon?

Certainly the main reason infants learn to speak so strangely is the way we talk to them from the day they're born. After months of having his/her chin tweaked accompanied by ridiculous "Goo-Goo's" and "Ga-Ga's," it's little wonder a baby's speech patterns become corrupted.

These meaningless prompts are then reinforced by an unnatural tone of voice. Baby hears a normal conversation in

[130]

the room; suddenly a large, grinning face hovers above the bassinet, speaking in a precious, over-inflected, honey-dripping lilt that should make any self-respecting adult sick to his stomach.

Then as Baby gets older, adults make learning to talk even more bizarre and difficult. As a caring paternal figure, you'll be shocked to hear good, solid English words and phrases inexplicably deformed for your infant's "benefit."

These do-gooding intruders, if not stopped, can leave permanent scars on your offspring's vocabulary.

Suffering Suffixes

For starters, all relatives passing through your home believe domesticated animals of the world must have a "y" or "ie" added to their names. Hence, the word horse becomes *horsey*; duck, *duckie*; kitten, *kitty*; hamster, *hammie* and so on. This perversion also applies to apparel. To wit: pajamas, *jammies*; boots, *booties*; diapers, *didies*; nightgown, *nightie*. Even wholesome food products are defamed for no apparent reason: vegetables become *veggies*; spaghetti, *sghettie*; scrambled eggs, *yeggies*; beans & franks, *beanie weenies*.

But all of the above has little impact when compared to infantile attempts to make bodily discharges sound like happy events: poopies, pee-pees, spit-em-ups, boogies, doo-doos, droolies, burpies and tee-tees.

Another confusing (and rather anti-feminist) development infants must endure is the addition of the title "Mister" to all of their stuffed toys: Mr. Bear, Mr. Lion, Mr. Moose, Mr. Clown, Mr. Potato Head, Mr. Spock, and so on. When Baby reaches kindergarten age, this could leave him/her with the attitude that it's okay to hug and kiss strangers as long as they introduce themselves as a Mister So-and-So. Tell your cutesy-pootsey, language-twisting friends and relatives this is not such a brainy idea.

Keep your ears peeled, Dad. There's still more linguistic poison in the air which will certainly contaminate your child's speech. These language-polluting visitors to your home may mean well, but they simply don't understand what this trash-talk can do.

The people who use the following words and phrases, for some reason, want your kid to sound cute instead of intelligent. Don't let them do this to your baby. Exercise your fatherly-duty and be on guard against the following popular abuses.

Proper Usage	Cutesy-Wutesy Perversion
Bottle	"Ba-Ba"
Man's Best Friend	"Gawgie"
Pasta in Tomato Sauce	"Sghettie"
Sleeptime	"Beddy-Bye"
Herd of Cattle	"Moo-Moos"

Proper Usage	Cutesy-Wutesy Perversion
Locomotive	"Choo-Choo"
Rabbit	"Bunny"
Good-night	"Nitey-Nite"
Toes	"Piggies"
Unacceptable Behavior	"No-No"
Bowel Movement	"Poo-Poo"
Altered State of Mind	"Cuckoo"

⌐   ⌐   ⌐   ⌐   ⌐

Swearing Baby In

There are certain words that babies seem to learn much quicker than others. I think you know which ones I'm referring to. These short, snappy sentences (usually with an exclamation point at the end) seem to come forth in times of great parental stress—against our wishes. In fact the words often seem to have a will of their own.

As a father, for instance, you could be sitting calmly watching your favorite major league team on television. It's a tie game in the top of the ninth when your relief pitcher throws a high curve ball that's belted into the left field bleachers for a grand slam. Out pops, "Aw, Sh__!" before you know it. Baby, sitting nearby, looks at you for a second, then echoes your sentiments precisely.

Why infants seem to grasp these popular expressions so quickly is a riddle. This is the same child you have been trying to teach "Dog" to for five months. Somehow, like the electronic fine-tuning on your radio and television, Baby automatically locks on to this frequency. Then he/she waits until important company arrives before presenting the most embarrassing reruns.

If your dinner guests drop their plates, tell them it must be something Baby picked up at Day Care. If your wife looks more guilty than embarrassed, remember that Mommies have their favorite expressions, too.

After the third or fourth episode, visiting relatives and close friends might begin to question the quality of your language instruction. You and your wife can blame it on R-rated videos all you want to. You can whine about what a curse it is, too. It doesn't matter. Your guests will instantly know what you're up to.

So what, exactly, can the two of you do?

Clamp off the naughtiness at its source? Issue a gag order? I don't think you can have Baby crawling around the dining room with zipped lips whether you opt for packing tape or an old-fashioned, tied-behind-the-head bandanna gag. Someone will notice for sure.

No, the only way to stem the blurt of bad words is to sterilize your own speech.

Before it's too late, get back in touch with "Drat!" "Shucks!" "Shazam!" "Golly!" "Fiddlesticks!" and "Gee-Willikers!" Being the designated father, you might select "Dad-blast-it!" or "Dad-burn!" as a personal favorite.

Yes sir, correcting your own habits is only one of the hurdles which step front and center during the lightning-quick changes of the walking/talking phase. When you feel you're in the midst of it, in a world of...hurt, so to speak, let this trusty guide be your guide.

When the time comes and you find yourself alone with an unstable, jabbering tot; if the ramble and the rumble leave you feeling hapless and helpless; if you seem to be losing your patience along with your mind; here's a special "Pop" Quiz which may help sharpen your fatherly skills...or at least give you a laugh or two while you're learning to cope.

You never know, one or two of these scenarios may help give you a fighting chance when you step into the infant-care ring. Put it in perspective. Walking/talking is the main event of Baby's young career as an up-and-coming human.

Consider it a challenge. See how many of the multiple choice questions you can answer correctly without peeking.

Go ahead, take a jab at it:

'Pop' Quiz Number Three:
"The Main Event"
Walking/Talking

Question:

Learning to walk, Baby somehow keeps stumbling and smashing his/her head on your brand-new Queen Anne dining group. Should you?

> (a) Put furniture in storage, temporarily replacing it with Styrofoam replicas
> (b) Put Baby in storage and replace him/her with a Styrofoam replica
> (c) Spend many hours (and dollars) installing do-it-yourself "infant guard" vinyl strips
> (d) Design a new infant-size roller derby helmet

The answer is
(a). This is the shrewd choice because not only will you save your furniture from certain destruction, but when you take it out of storage in twenty years, its value will have appreciated considerably. Forget answer (b), your wife is bound to notice. (c) would take so many man-hours to complete you would have to quit your job (and then you couldn't afford to pay off the furniture debt). Ditto answer (d).

Question:

You've had a fun day saving your staggering tyke from multiple disaster. A few minutes before Mommy gets home, Baby mysteriously trips over a ball of lint, crashes into a wall unit, triggering a deadly chain reaction which claims your wife's priceless porcelain doll collection. Should you?

> (a) Let the dog in, telling him to lie down near the scene of the crime
> (b) Get the dustpan, whisk broom and a very large tube of super-glue
> (c) Confess your negligence and beg for mercy
> (d) Grab your pillow and blanket and plan to spend the next several nights in the dog's house (that is, if he'll still have you)

The answer is
(none of the above). A trick question, to be sure, but perhaps that will help concerned fathers remember the point. You'd have to be a disloyal creep to choose (a) and forever lose the respect of your best friend. How about (b)? Not enough time, sorry. Only a nerd would select (c), causing (d) to follow automatically. No, the correct response for mature fathers is to bury the evidence, check for fingerprints, call the police and insurance companies and tell them you've been robbed.

Question:

You and your crawling ten-month-old are alone on a cold winter day. She keeps pulling up to the hearth, inches from a blazing fire. Should you?

> (a) Put out the fire and turn up the furnace
> (b) Go get fire extinguisher from garage, keep it by your easy chair, just in case
> (c) Detach smoke alarm from wall and strap it to Baby's back
> (d) Tell your child (in a no-nonsense) tone that the colorful flames are hot, and they will fry her little piggy toes if she gets any closer

The answer is
(d). (a) is okay, except your gas bill is high enough already. The logic of (b) and (c) may be appealing at first glance; too bad they're based on reaction instead of prevention. However, since warning Baby probably won't work the first ten times, it might be wise to keep (b) and (c) in mind.

Question:

On your morning off, you and your two-year-old stop by elderly Uncle Bob's and the three of you go for a walk in the park. Wobbly grand uncle and baby nephew, holding hands, trek to the top of a grassy hill. You turn your head, Bob's cane slips on a wet patch and he and Baby tumble head-over-heels to the park benches below. Should you?

> (a) Admire Bob's somersault form and ask for the name of his gymnastics instructor
> (b) Shout, "Last one to the bottom's a rotten egg!"

(c) Grab Bob's cane, snap it in two over your knee, then check to see if anybody's bones have snapped also

(d) Run up, clap vigorously as you tell them how proud you are—theirs is the most realistic impression of Jack and Jill you've ever seen

The answer is

(c). Why not (a)? You're a new parent—you don't have time. (b) injects competition into the scene— unnecessary. (d) is a thoughtful gesture, but the welfare of your kin makes (c) the priority. (You can buy Bob a new cane later.)

Question:

You come home late from a hard day at the office and find Aunt Ethel camped out by the crib, teaching your little boy how to say cute things like "boo-boo" and "pee-pee." Should you?

(a) Politely state that those words are slightly silly and you'd prefer it if Baby didn't learn them

(b) Inform Auntie that hearing "pee-pee" makes you sick to your stomach, then prove it on her robe

(c) Smack Aunt Ethel in the face and tell her to mind her own business

(d) Say, "Son, the correct usage for those words is 'injury' and 'urinate.' Please make a mental note."

The answer is,
of course, (d). Because answer (a) would cause family friction, (b) would create a scene and (c) would provoke a lawsuit... (d) is the only possible alternative.

Question:

It's just you and your offspring on an October evening during the World Series. Baby is standing by the television, babbling continuously and blocking the picture. Should you?

> (a) Enroll Baby in Broadcasting school
> (b) Tell Baby to quit crowding the screen or you'll show 'em up-close what a real brush-back pitch feels like
> (c) Look for rope and a roll of duct tape
> (d) Scream, "You're outta here!" and escort infant to his/her room

The answer is
(b). This is the thoughtful solution because it would help prepare Baby for later encounters in Little League. (a) would require your wife's approval and that takes time. On the other hand, your wife would likely disapprove of (c) if she walks in unexpectedly. Similar to (b), the answer (d) also teaches sound baseball fundamentals, but goes a bit too far.

Question:

Reverend Thomas is relaxing in your recliner on a fund-raising visit. Baby falls at his feet, accidentally spits on his loafers and exclaims, "Sh_t and Shinola!" Should you?

(a) Jump up and say, "Darn! The parrot's loose again!"

(b) Throw infant a drool rag and order him/her to buff 'em up right

(c) Smile, tilt your head and ask, "Did you say something, reverend?"

(d) Get out your checkbook and fill in triple digits

The answer is,
undoubtedly, (d). You can try all the others, (a), (b) and (c), but you may as well embrace reality and put your money where Baby's mouth is.

Question:

You've been trying to teach your thirteen-month-old daughter to say "Daddy" for six months. One evening, your next-door-neighbor, Jerry, walks in and Baby rushes to his arms, squealing, "Daddy! Daddy! Daddy!" Should you?

(a) Hire a private detective

(b) Lie down in the street and wait for a bus

(c) Ask Jerry if he'd like to move in with you

(d) Ask Jerry if he'd like a stuffed doggie up his nose

The answer is
(a). Feeling depressed, you might choose (b) as a first reaction, but think of the mess. (c) appears quite generous and sophisticated, but it's simply another messy solution to an already complex problem. Less sophisticated is (d), besides

the fact that it would accomplish little. With (a) you're at least trying something constructive.

Score ten points for each correct answer.
Then add it up and look for your rating below.

Walking/Talking Pop Quiz
"The Main Event"

Score	Official Rating
0	Unconscious
10	Bum
20	Punch Drunk Pug
30	Rank Amateur
40	Flyweight
50	Contender
60	Club Champ
70	Heavyweight Hero
80	THE GREATEST

Cheer up if your quiz grade is lower than you'd like it to be. All the walking/talking clash does is set a good pace for your serious training. Till they get their stamina up, a lot of new fathers tend to fade in the late rounds. Remember, life is the true test, the real match, and you'll have many opportunities to reclaim your self-esteem.

Baby's first steps and first words represent merely the beginning of a long and fascinating learning phase for both of you. The challenges ahead will demand your total commitment to retaining sanity, ducking abuse and sidestepping a flurry of painful kidney punches.

As a dedicated Father/Caretaker, you're about to discover the terrors of toddlerhood lurking just around the corner. Don't rush it. Once your child reaches twenty-four months (give or take a couple), you'll be looking back on his/her breast-feeding days with nothing but hungry nostalgia.

Chapter ten

Holy Moses! The Ten Commandments of 21st Century Infant Care

⌐   ⌐   ⌐   ⌐   ⌐   ⌐   ⌐

In *Keeping Your Toddler on Track till Mommy Gets Back*, we unveiled the ancient and mystical TEN COMMAND-MENTS OF TODDLER TRANTRUMS, unearthed in the ruins of Pompeii by the Clearing Skies Press archaeological team. Now, we introduce an even more startling discovery from 16th century France, THE TEN COMMANDMENTS OF 21st CEN-TURY INFANT CARE. For nearly six hundred years this incredible parchment scroll lay protected inside a leather tube behind a loose brick in the wall of a cottage in Amboise, France.

[145]

The infant care commandments are most startling because 1) They exist, 2) They are future-formatted for the 21st century, and 3) They were apparently created by brilliant Italian artist-inventor, Leonardo da Vinci; not that he wasn't a capable man, but he is thought by historians to be gay.

So what would he know about father-infant care in any century? Well, we're not sure, but since Leonardo basically invented and detail-sketched the helicopter, submarine, airplane and automobile five-hundred years ahead of time, we're going to give the guy the benefit of the doubt.

The Ten Commandments of 21st Century Infant Care

1. Thou shalt have no other babies before me, and more important, no carefree adult pursuits after I am among thee.

2. Thou shalt not place images of my birth before frightened workmates just because thy love me, worship me and serve me above all others till the end of thy days.

3. Thou shalt not take the name of thy Lord in vain though thy tongue be severely tempted every time I giveth thee profound piles of poop and faithful puddles of pee over the next one thousand days & nights.

4. Remember thy Baby's birth-day (and thy wife's birth-day) and keep both holy forevermore and celebrate both blessed events with lavish gifts to the limits of thy credit-worthiness.

5. As mother and father, thy shalt be honored with ceaseless toil and thy days shalt be long upon the earth, verily, until the blessed day of my college graduation.

6. Thou shalt not kill...even the vast and virulent hordes of relatives who invade your living room, raid your ice box and cast you out of your den and away from your personal computer and television.

7. Thou shalt not commit adultery...nor commit any normal, loving act of marital intimacy whilst thy infant be 50 cubits or nearer, for I shalt call out to thee again and again and thy shalt suffer the gravest form of coitus interruptus ad infinitum.

8. Thou shalt not steal...lo, after the sun goeth down, cherished minutes of quiet and relaxation abetted by adult beverages, as care of me, day and night, requireth the dull, sober faithfulness of a desert camel.

9. Thou shalt not bear false witness against thy neighbor when thy neighbor knoweth thou hast a squalling infant nightly in the pre-dawn time before the sun cometh up.

10. Thou shalt not covet thy neighbor's childless house, nor covet thy neighbor's cute, babyless wife, as thy cherish thy own wife, tho she be cursed with a surplus of poundage which abideth unto her frame.

Chapter eleven

Fun and Games for Fathers and Other Fools

⌐   ⌐   ⌐   ⌐   ⌐   ⌐   ⌐   ⌐

"Let the Games Begin!"
—said the master of ceremonies,
prior to introducing the day's first
Christian to the lions

Just as in ancient Rome, when innocent victims took their last trembling steps toward the gaping maw of a savage beast...you, my friend, must learn to play the "games" that fill your demanding audience's daily entertainment quota. Are the odds against you? Yes, decidedly. Still you must reckon with Baby's lusty appetite for unique, exciting, even exotic diversions. Either that, or like the less nimble performers in the Colosseum...you'll suffer very cruel consequences.

An Act of Desperation

Since you're in the spotlight and trapped into playing these so-called "games," how do you learn them and where do you start? Since this greedy audience-of-one leaves you no easy exit...how do you get the inside information you need to perform up to your usual manly standards?

I don't know about you, but I had trouble walking up to my wife and casually asking her to teach me how to play "Pat-a-Cake." Instead I secretly listened and watched, privately making notes during mommy-offspring play. That sophisticated brand of information-age research helped me put together a modest yet reliable lineup of infant routines.

These timeless bits are both entertaining and absurdly simple—perfect for proud but painfully ignorant mommy-impostors like you and me.

The point is, you can learn these classic diversions here and practice on your own without real Mommy's knowledge. This will eliminate sloppy, embarrassing rehearsals not meant for prime family time.

Then, even though you will still look and feel perfectly idiotic, you can go about your business with some degree of confidence and dignity. Baby will respect your initiative if nothing else. One day your wife may catch you in the act and watch your performance with a knowing smirk (perhaps even a giggle or two)...but you won't have to put up with outright laughter.

Of course laughter is the only goal when you're engrossed in the hazardous business of entertaining infants. You want to keep the yuks coming at any cost. This requires a smooth delivery, perfect timing, great stage presence and most important, a dependable repertoire of rotating gags. After all, you're following a tough act named Mommy. That makes Baby no pushover for an easy chuckle.

A Most Demanding Audience

Picture yourself as a young, hardworking stand-up comic looking for a break. You're struggling to make a name for yourself yet your agent sticks you with a weekend gig in some low-rent strip joint because you need the work. You take the stage in front of a noisy, uncooperative audience (Baby) who looks altogether insulted by your appearance.

Quickly, the mood takes a nasty turn. Discontent shifts from restless cooing to abusive babble. You realize this crowd has mayhem on its mind. To them, you're simply a cheap imitation taking up space and time. What the crowd wants to know is, where's the real thing (Mommy)? What the audience came to see is soft, lovable, familiar femininity. In comparison, you're loud, relatively unknown and totally boring from a breast-feeding standpoint—plus you have hairy arms and scratchy whiskers.

[151]

But, believe it or not, you can overcome these liabilities and still make a show of it. The secret is audience participation. You want to get Baby so involved in the action that he/she forgets exactly who you aren't.

At the same time, you'll be developing your own winning style of showmanship. Before long your precise, polished, uniquely paternal talent will have this surly crowd jumping out of its high chair, screaming for encores.

Or go in unpracticed if you like. As long as you're fully prepared to be disgraced, booed out of the room with (real) egg on your face and written off as a hopeless has-been.

The choice is yours. Study the following carefully-screened activities and you'll soon be on the road to rave reviews. Many, especially the traditional slapstick routines, go over so well they've become public domain. Passed down from mother to mother over generations, these little amusements seem to click with an infant's warped sense of humor. I have no idea why. But after you've become a slick-performing, in-the-know pappy—you'll find yourself repeating them *dad infinitum*.

I remember it fondly. Sitting attentively in her high chair, with spastic hand-claps and squeals, my sixteen-month-old daughter once requested alternating Pat-a-Cake and Peek-a-Boo for two hours straight. Encored into exhaustion, I brought the magic of milk, animal crackers and homemade Mommy fudge into the act.

The audience only screamed for more.

The Classic Repertoire

for your eyes only, a listing of patented infant routines passed down through the centuries, specially updated for today's fun-loving, physically-fit dads:

Peek-a-Boo

Location:	anywhere...changing table to playpen to couch to closet
Helpful Props:	burping cloth, bath towel, pillow, sheet of paper, wall or door...any handy opaque object big enough to cover your face

This all-time favorite qualifies as a top-of-the-chart request by infants around the world. Mainly what *Peek-a-Boo* has going for it is the element of surprise. Over-indulged, bored infants love surprises. All you need do is put a prop between the two of you, then suddenly remove it, revealing a goofball, mouth-open expression of simulated shock. Just add a quick falsetto "Peek-a-Boo!" as you tilt forward, eyes bulging, toward Baby's face.

That's it. Then repeat until your voice and facial muscles give out.

Pat-a-Cake

Location: preferably, a seating arrangement where you and Baby can face each other and touch hands

Helpful Props: just your imagination unless you'd like to add an optional marking pen, pair of aprons and/or pizza pan

Originally intended to be early training for girls and boys practicing time-honored trades as innkeepers and bakers. Now for everyone, especially future pizza chain executives. There are a million variations to the words in Pat-a-Cake, but what follows is official. Memorize them now and forever—otherwise you will never pass security checks at playgrounds and PTA meetings:

"Pat-a-cake, pat-a-cake, baker's man!
Bake me a cake as fast as you can.
Roll it and pat it and mark it with a 'B.'
Throw it in the oven for Baby and me."

Sing in mindless sing-song fashion, alternating hand-claps with Baby and yourself in staccato rhythm. After the first two verses, change to rolling and patting motions, then mark a big "B" in the air in front of Baby's nose. Then stuff the imaginary cake into Baby's midriff.

I know, I know. Compared to Peek-a-Boo, Pat-a-Cake is pretty complicated. But very impressive if you get it right. So keep trying. In no time, you'll be a master Caker. And Baby will think you're cooler than chocolate pudding.

Eye Blinker

Location: same as Pat-a-Cake, face-to-face

Helpful Props: in case of accident it might be nice to
                      have eyewash and nose drops on hand.
                      Sterilized gloves are good, too

Another classic test of your father credentials, Eye Blinker combines insipid two-word phrases with parental finger pokes. The original purpose of this little pastime was to teach Baby about facial anatomy. But beware: a little lesson about flailing/bobbing infants, lack of finger coordination and severe eye injury could be the result.

To perform Eye Blinker properly, simply touch the appropriate infant body part as you repeat: "Eye-Blinker (left eye)...Tom-Tinker (right eye)...Nose-Dropper...Mouth-Eater...Chin-Chopper, Chin-Chopper, Chin-Chopper. A swooping, chin-tickling flourish along with Chin-Chopper usually wows the crowd.

Horsey

Location: Daddy's knee

Helpful Props: for those who insist on realism: jockey
                      silks, whip, saddle, reins and
                      The Daily Racing Form

[155]

A worthy rival of Peek-a-Boo, Horsey has long been a father-favorite. It has a masculine sort of appeal to it, and of course babies love it too. Or maybe they just like the idea of testing Daddy's fragile knee joints with an imaginary whip in their hands. However you perceive it, Horsey is a bona fide classic, yet a matter of personal style. Plus you can "walk," "trot," "canter" or "gallop" for years if your knees and ankles stay sound.

Personally, I prefer a touch of classical music as a background. At a slow humming pace, The William Tell Overture is a nice choice, especially if you can make trumpet sounds. Then after you hum to a crescendo—and pause—lift Baby high in the air, shaking him/her gently as you make a cartoonish horse whinny.

You can bet on Horsey. It's a sure winner.

This Little Pig

Location: favorites are changing table, bathtub

Helpful Props: barefoot baby

A well-worn rerun, this slapstick number still captures its share of admirers. It spawned "piggy-toes" as a universal part of baby language, and heaven help us, probably promoted a bad image for pork. But to do it, just tug in turn on each of Baby's toes, starting with the big one. Finish with a theatrical tug and falsetto squeal on the little toe.

In case you've forgotten the words your mother used when she did *This Little Pig* with you:

> *"This little pig went to market;*
> *This little pig stayed home;*
> *This little pig had roast beef;*
> *This little pig had none. (pause)*
> *This little pig cried, 'Wee, wee, wee!' all the way home."*

How did this piece of schlock get to be so popular? Well, I guess there's just no accounting for the average infant's taste (or lack of it).

Itsy-Bitsy Spider

Location: facing baby

Helpful Props: for the dedicated realist, a watering can and sunlamp

Little Miss Muffet is tame compared to this colorful, action-packed, arachnid thriller. First, spread your fingers spider-like and touch your left thumb to right pinkie. Then in a slow upward crawl, rotate to opposite digits (alternating left thumb/right pinkie to right thumb/left pinkie), singing:

> *"The Itsy-Bitsy Spider crawled up the waterspout."*

Next, wiggle fingers downward like falling rain (or use watering can), singing:

> *"Down came the rain and washed the spider out."*

[157]

Make imaginary sun rays (or use sunlamp), singing:

"Out came the sun and dried up all the rain."

Repeat thumb-pinkie spider crawl, singing:

"Then Itsy-Bitsy spider went up the spout again."
(End)

If this classic version seems to lack a powerful finale, you might consider improvisation. For instance, a lunging make-believe spider bite to the neck, with sound effects. Of course this decision may depend on your Baby's individual age, sense of humor and nervous system.

Pillow Plop

Location: over bed, sofa or plush carpeting. Definitely avoid tile floors, concrete patios and rocky beaches

Helpful Props: trampoline

An up-and-comer, Pillow Plop is attracting a growing audience among time-pressed fathers and infants. All you have to do is position offspring a foot or two over the target, let go and shout, "Geronimo!"

Now doesn't that sound like quick and simple fun? Just take time to utilize an extra-large pillow, a good, firm grip and proper aim...so Baby's soft plop doesn't become a splat.

Setting the Stage for Itsy-Bitsy Spider

Pinch-a-Cheek

Location: changing table

Helpful Props: baby's behind, metronome

Emerging research indicates this musical number quietly achieved cult status in the last decades of the 20th century. Not surprisingly, enlightened dads have gotten into the act increasingly in recent years. Mothers recognized centuries ago that babies have dual sets of appealingly plump cheeks. Both beg to be pinched, patted and squeezed.

When you take the time to add a good sense of rhythm (or metronome) and a whimsical tone to each squeeze...you can literally make music with these babies.

Put together your own composition. Then pretend the changing table is your stage. Or create a festive atmosphere with circus calliope sounds. The main thing to remember about Pinch-a-Cheek is only to play *after* you change the diaper.

Dropsy

Location: crib, playpen, scooter, high chair...
                         any elevated site

Helpful Props: every toy in the house that you feel
                      like picking up in a two-minute period

Compared to other gaming customs, Dropsy is totally unique. First, it isn't a game you play with Baby. "Dropsy" is Baby's way of playing games with you. Often, you'll find yourself in the middle of a game before you realize you're a participant. The familiar pattern goes like this:

Step 1: Baby drops toy, you pick it up.

Step 2: Baby drops two toys, you pick them up.

Step 3: Baby flings five toys, you stoop for two while Baby throws three more.

Step 4: Baby sweeps across high chair/crib rail, dumps an entire pile on the floor while you fetch.

Step 5: Baby waits while you reload location.

Step 6: Baby drops toy.

(Repeat sequence.)

Clearly, calling Dropsy a game is shallow thinking at best. Rather, it's the infant kingdom's subtle version of psychological revenge, a seemingly innocent diversion designed to torment parents since the beginning of time.

Thinking of cold and hurt and hungry and afraid... they'll make us pay for bringing them into this scene in the first place. And watching us, they'll have a very entertaining time doing it.

Please note that I am not personally sanctioning the somewhat questionable activity which makes up the upcoming final entry in The Classic Repertoire list of games. It's merely being passed along to help keep the modern father informed and up-to-date regarding potential techniques in gamesmanship. If someone *were* to play *Daddy's Special Hide-and-Seek,* here's how it might work.

Daddy's Special Hide-and-Seek

Location: in an approved baby-safe room only

Helpful Props: Record/play CD drive or tape recorder

You might also call this cheap gag, "Hide-and-Trick" or "Keep Looking, Can't You Hear Me?"

Before you start, do your best to plan for a few minutes of quiet time when Mommy is out. Naptime may be your only opportunity. Unplug the phone, lock the family room door, then prepare your recording with care. Be certain there are no behind-the-door snoops or interruptions. With this routine, you can't afford to be caught in the act.

When everything is set up, pretend you are alone with Baby, talking calmly. You shouldn't need to write a script. But you might want to jot down a few notes if you start stumbling over words. Be natural. Use soothing, familiar phrases certain to make Baby feel at ease:

"Come see Daddy, sweetheart/pal. Over here."
"Keep looking...you're getting closer."
"Can't you hear me?"
"You're on the right track. Almost there now."
Slowly, melodically (as from a distant hilltop):

[162]

"S-h-a-n-n-o-n...M-i-c-h-a-e-l...J-e-n-n-i-f-e-r..."

Repeat above phrases till your conscience takes command (or you run out of smart things to say).

Later, during a Sunday afternoon baby-sitting assignment (after rigorous soul-searching) you can start the game of hide-and-seek. Only if you're sure you have no sense of shame...place auto-reverse recorder/repeat-play CD player and Baby in baby-safe room and close the door. Next, order a pizza, pop a brew, then relax in your recliner and enjoy an NFL doubleheader.

Tips You Can Get Away With

Lord knows, infant-entertaining is demanding sport. Doing it while you're driving is one of life's great challenges. The fact is, ordinary infant-type recreation needs to be adjusted to be successful in your automobile.

Before you turn the key you can feel that the space is awkward and confining. You glance back and see your tortured offspring strapped in more securely than a just-captured escaped convict. You realize even though you're in the driver's seat, you have no control. What can a Dad do?

Used wisely, your audio system may meet with audience approval for a few minutes. But games like *Horsey, Eye Blinker* and even *Peek-a-Boo* can be downright dangerous. What else is there? Briefly, here are a few helpful travel ideas to, well, get you going:

Count the Moo Moo's*:

Of course your infant can't count—which in this game gives you carte blanche to lie, cheat and generally confuse Baby into a state of passive submission. When you see a herd of cattle, say, "Hey, Babe. Check out the moo-moos. How many do you see?" Wait for a second, then rattle off a series of random numbers. Then tell Baby it's his/her turn to count. If there's no immediate response, laugh heartily and say, "Sorry, Babycakes. You're a loser."

Which brings up an important point about infant games in general. Namely, it's a lot more fun to be on the winning side.

Perhaps, though, it might be fairer to base the game on cow color instead. You know, "Look! Look! There's a black spotted one...can you tell Daddy what colors those are?" Or "See! There's a brown moo moo over there." Or "Whoa! Look at that black cow on top of that brown cow next to the fence. What color do black and brown make together?"

*"Tabulate the Bovines" to those who prefer proper English

It may occur to you that one requirement for playing this visual type of car game is that Baby must be sitting high enough to see out. Most babies, being sensitive about their lack of height anyway, may balk upon seeing artificial lifts introduced under their car seat. And there is also a question of safety in raising your offspring to a point where he/she becomes more vulnerable in a crash.

A small, flat suitcase*, then, becomes the perfect solution as long as it is strapped securely under Baby's car seat.

[164]

Because it is a natural travel item, your offspring won't find the suitcase offensive, especially when you explain to Baby that every stitch of his/her clothing is inside. Just be careful not to raise your little one so high that his/her head touches the roof liner. Potholes and speed bumps then tend to cause extreme discomfort, particularly to babies still plagued by that pulsating soft spot on their crown.

*consult your insurance provider and pediatrician prior to suitcase use

THE ESSENTIAL LONG-DISTANCE AUTO TRAVEL KIT FOR INFANTS

Do your utmost to keep these indispensible items close-at-hand. Tuck them under the front seat, in door bins and visor flaps. Don't hide them in the trunk.

When your offspring decides to start driving *you* crazy, you don't want to be caught having to pull over and pop the trunk lid, then risk your life on the side of the highway fumbling around like some dope in the dark.

1. Earplugs
2. One dozen *Mother Goose* books
3. Pacifier
4. *Playboy* joke book**

5. Full audio library of infant "listen 'n learn"
CDs or cassette tapes

6. Set of dice**

7. State-of-the-art cattle prod

8. Deck of cards**

9. *The New York Times***

10. Complete set of hand puppet characters
from *Sesame Street*, *The Disney Channel*, *The
Howdy Doody Show* and *Looney Tunes* cartoons

11. Flight bag containing multiple disguises
(a la Peter Sellers in the *Pink Panther* films)

12. A copy of the old bestseller, *How to
Hypnotize Yourself and Others*

13. An infant look-alike voodoo doll

**preferred by parents, but attractive option for the more mature infant

The Last Word on Gaming

The end of a rugged road trip...after a long-running
tour at home...these are not the best times to properly assess
your performance as a Master Gamester. But when the curtain finally closes on a full day of tending to and caring for
that complex, playful, growing miracle you helped produce,
chances are, you won't be too sensitive about criticism, good
or bad.

You'll likely find yourself more concerned about losing control than worrying about winning style. Games aside, these lessons of life are hard-won and lasting.

Then, just when you think you've learned infant care well—on your way to achieving respect as a father-per-former—old Father Time steps in and changes all the rules. Your baby is suddenly twenty-something (months) old and ready for toddlerhood.

That will be the time to pause, reflect and remember you're not the only party in the spotlight. After all, you and I and Mom and family and a worldwide, multi-billion dollar infant industry...we're in this game of chance together.

And we're all holding the same hand.

Toddlerhood...
State of Mind, State of Terror

Chapter twelve

The Terror of Toddler Care: a (Scary) Peek Ahead

⌐   ⌐   ⌐   ⌐   ⌐   ⌐   ⌐

Oh, a trouble's a ton, or a trouble's an ounce,
Or a trouble is what you make it.
And it isn't the fact that you're hurt that counts,
But only how did you take it?

—Poet Edmund Vance Cooke

Take heart, o wise paternal leader. Your journey into the badlands of toddlerdom rides swiftly on the winds of change. But since you're charging ahead as a veteran commander of the baby rebellion, you have no reason to fear trouble. True? Well, as with practically every question concerning children, the answer is *Yes* and *No*. Yes, you're a valuable, experienced member of Troop Parenting, a bullet-dodging survivor of the hellfire action that comes with frontline infant care.

You know what dirty trench duty in the diaper brigade is all about. You know what it's like to wear vomit on your lapel. Serving breakfast, you know the feeling of tripping over a stuffed animal and falling head-first into a warming dish full of gooey scrambled eggs. Always battling to be a better dad, YOU KNOW how to saddle up and soldier on even when you're tired, discouraged and getting shot down with every infant-care move you make.

What YOU DON'T KNOW is that compared to the minor skirmishes you've had with Baby, taking care of your toddler is like The Battle of Little Big Horn, and you're on the side of General Custer.

Charging Ahead Against All Odds: What You Know (and Don't Know) About Daddy-Toddler Care

YOU KNOW   your incredible laddy-boy is growing insanely fast and and that week after week, he not only gets bigger, but quicker on his feet, both physically and mentally

YOU DON'T KNOW   how long you can keep up with him physically or mentally, but at least he'll be smaller than you for a long time to come

YOU KNOW   "No!" is becoming your toddler darling's favorite word, more so with each passing day

YOU DON'T KNOW   if she thinks "No!" is *your* favorite word, but the more she grows into toddlerhood, the more you're forced to use it

YOU KNOW   as the months march by, whenever Mommy's out-of-town, you and your toddler son, also known as Insomniac Jack, have ridiculous naptime battles that take too much time and energy

YOU DON'T KNOW   when he will finally shut his eyes and nod off, but you're ready to collapse by his crib and nod off now—without the aid of a pacifier or bedtime story

YOU KNOW   that weaning time is here and that taking her beloved bottle away from your toddler girl will result in weeks of squalling fits and screaming tirades

YOU DON'T KNOW   what the neighbors will think about the squalling and screaming—you just hope you can make yourself stop at some point

YOU KNOW   at the age of 24 months your daughter outgrows her latest set of embroidered, lace-trimmed coveralls in approximately 52 days

YOU DON'T KNOW   how you ever lived this long without setting foot in a second-hand clothing store, but now you personally know the owners of five and which ones give the best discounts on toddler apparel

YOU KNOW   you shouldn't expect your son to learn the meaning of "sharing" just because he'll be a toddler soon

[171]

YOU DON'T KNOW   specifically about his ability to share his favorite toddler toys, but you know he's shared a half-dozen colds with you since he was four months old

YOU KNOW   that toddlers and tantrums go together like a snifter of Grand Marnier and a fine cigar

YOU DON'T KNOW   at the end of a typical father-toddler week, how much Friday night snifting and smoking it will take to ease the trauma of umpteen toddler tantrums

YOU KNOW   bragging is an important part of your parental rights package, and bragging about your toddler is a 24-hour/7-Days-a-Week compulsion whether you have a girl or a boy, frequent or occasional toddler-sitting duties

YOU DON'T KNOW   if your office mates wish you'd get lost when you open up another package of toddler pictures in their cubicles, but the groans are getting louder

YOU KNOW   you'll look back on your child's magical infancy with wistfulness and affection someday

YOU DON'T KNOW   today, what your toddlerette is doing grunting in the corner, but she smells less than magical

YOU KNOW   you have inner fears about that great landmark event of toddlerhood—potty training

YOU DON'T KNOW   when the time comes, if you'll be too pooped to Pop or if your toddler will be too Popped to poop, but you figure it will all come out okay in the end

[172]

A Little "Pop" in Your Bat Goes a Long Way with Toddlers

"Play Ball!" You've been in and out of the lineup for months, but now it's time to take your childcare skills to a new level. On a moment's notice, Coach Mommy expects you to jump off the bench and pinch-hit competently. The star of the game—your crafty toddler—atop a mound of contradictions, constantly throws you curves, surprises you with a blazing tantrum one minute, then changes up everything by offering a sweet smile and hug the next.

You're not certain how all of this will play out, but you know everyone on the home team is counting on you.

Most of the time, the female caregivers around you like what they see. Your stance is solid and you've displayed good hand-eye coordination, wiping the plate clean after feedings; flashing speed while running to the store for formula. You've learned a lot observing your wife's professional approach, plus your own style shows potential in clutch situations.

All you have to do now is remember to think less like a man and more like a Mommy. Yes, the male point of view is important in infant care and toddler care. At least it's important to you and me. What women *really* think about our input is another story. Yet, up to a limit, we daddies can do our own childcare thing and not worry about female critiques.

<u>Last-Minute Word to the Wise: Be Wise, Be Not a Wise-Guy</u>. Toward toddlers especially, if you let your confident

masculine attitude go a bit too far, you might find yourself striking out on a nasty change-up with a full count and training pants loaded. That would stink. And foul (smelling) balls just won't do when the home team needs you. Your game plan? Don't worry about swinging for the fences. As clean-up man, all you have to do is spank a dribbler through the hole and take a wide turn around the changing table.

The home crowd will love you as long as you don't act like an obnoxious, hairy-chested know-it-all. Get too carried away, too full of yourself, too far from your true field of expertise...there's a chance you could be booed permanently back to the bench.

Take a humble, helpful approach and everyone will be happier for it. Get in touch with your feminine side, keep your weight back and wait on the right pitch. Sooner or later, you'll be a bona fide hit.

Before you know it, toddler time will fly by and you'll be living a smooth preschooler lifestyle. At that point in the contest do you dust off your cleats, slip into your conception uniform, and perform (once again) like an all-star stud? Do you intentionally walk back to a time of hard labor, sleepless nights and screwball infant-care schedules?

Well, all a fellow double-daddy can say is, no matter how you and your mate choose to engage the game of life, that one is forever a big-time, major-league decision.

Pop's Down-and-Dirty, Tuneful Top 30

⌐ ⌐ ⌐ ⌐ ⌐ ⌐ ⌐

As a dutiful dad (whether struggling or in full command of the moment), you need all of the background support you can call upon. Every resource, reference material, mood-altering aid in the book. That's why this helpful guide boasts the following custom-tailored Pop's music list for your personal use.

It's a beautifully condensed, unique, no-nonsense audio library to help you—in every desperate situation—match the music to the mood.

[175]

When you and Baby are alone...when you find yourself free-falling into infant-care despair...if the bottom's dropped out and you're left with nothing but the shaft...well, that's when you need a whole lot more than elevator music to lift your spirits and put your feelings into perspective.

Grouped by chapter heading for quick reference, these selections represent a decidedly peculiar yet curiously satisfying blend of "Pop" stylings. Just like your relationship with Baby (often disturbing, always unpredictable), these diverse melodies seem to grow on you. Whether you like it or not.

So stock your CD and/or MP3 player, slip your offspring a pair of (compact) headphones, turn up the volume and put these tunes to the test.

POP'S DOWN-AND-DIRTY, TUNEFUL TOP 30

Chapter One
Birthing Suites Ain't Made for Babies

1) *Makin' Whoopee* . . . . .Dr. John
2) *April Showers* . . . . .Al Jolson
3) *Tired of Waiting for You* . . . . .The Kinks
4) *Born to Be Wild* . . . . .Steppenwolf

Chapter Two
Home from the Hospital (a Star is Born)

Chapter Three
Poopies: a Sticky Situation from Top to Bottom

Chapter Four
Feeding a Face Only a Father Could Love

Chapter Five
Propagating Toys or Things That Go Hump in the Night

15) *The Nutcracker Suite* . . . . .Tchaikovsky
16) *Return to Sender* . . . . .Elvis Presley

Chapter Six
Infant Tyranny—a Devil of a Dilemma

17) *Purple Haze* . . . . .Jimi Hendrix
18) *I'm No Angel* . . . . .Gregg Allman

Chapter Seven
Day Care Litters and Baby Sitter Jitters

19) *We Gotta Get Out of This Place* . . . The Animals
20) *Take Good Care of My Baby* . . . . . . .Bobby Vee

Chapter Eight
Secrets to Avoiding Infant Abuse

21) *Help!* . . . . The Beatles
22) *Hit the Road Jack* . . . . Ray Charles

Chapter Nine
First Steps / First Words: The Leaning Tower of Babble

Chapter Ten
The Ten Commandments of Infant Care

Chapter Eleven
Fun and Games for Fathers and Other Fools

Chapter Twelve
The Terror of Toddler Care

Thank You, Thank You, Thank You

So many people with such good advice (if not good, then well-intentioned), there's no way in the world one can thank them all. But with a large leap of faith, I'll see what I can do. Please forgive me if I forget you.

Thank you to Susan and Meghan for inspiring me to record a tenderfoot's views in the first place. To Shannon, born in the car, still giving me gray hairs, thank you for being you. Without the three of you....

Mom, I wish, have wished, you were around to see this in print, and then maybe we could sit down and talk about a million other things. As always, your sense of humor (generously given) sets the tone in my work. I miss you.

Genuine appreciation to Jason Snape for (again) creating excellent illustrations, this time for an important, new-look edition. Ed Cahill, you're a great friend and you've turned out another sensational cover design.

Thanks to all at Independent Publishers Group for your help and wise counsel, to the good people at Color House Graphics for another fine printing, and to Harry Zegers at *Pregnancy* magazine for helping promote us. To USA Baby store owners, merci beaucoup for the support and orders.

Lastly, thank you to all the thousands of new dads (and moms) who have read and enjoyed the regular edition of *Keeping the Baby Alive till Your Wife Gets Home*. Without you this edition could never have happened.